Everyman's Poetry

*Everyman, I will go with thee,
and be thy guide*

Emily Dickinson

Selected and edited by HELEN McNEIL

University of East Anglia

EVERYMAN

J. M. Dent · London

Introduction and other critical apparatus
© J. M. Dent 1997

All rights reserved

J. M. Dent
Orion Publishing Group
Orion House
5 Upper St Martin's Lane
London WC2H 9EA

Typeset by Deltatype Ltd, Birkenhead, Merseyside
Printed in Great Britain by
The Guernsey Press Co. Ltd, Guernsey, C. I.

British Library Cataloguing-in-Publication
Data is available on request

ISBN 0 460 87895 6

Contents

Note on the Author and Editor   viii
Chronology of Dickinson's Life and Times   x.
Introduction   xviii
A Note on This Text   xxvii

Poems

  67 Success is counted sweetest 3
187 How many times these low feet staggered – 3
193 I shall know why – when Time is over – 4
199 I'm "wife" – I've finished that – 4
211 Come slowly – Eden! 5
214 I taste a liquor never brewed – 5
216 Safe in their Alabaster Chambers – (two versions) 6
225 Jesus! thy Crucifix 7
228 Blazing in Gold and quenching in Purple 7
239 "Heaven" – is what I cannot reach! 7
241 I like a look of Agony, 8
243 I've known a Heaven, like a Tent – 8
248 Why – do they shut Me out of Heaven? 9
249 Wild Nights – Wild Nights! 9
250 I shall keep singing! 10
251 Over the fence – 10
252 I can wade Grief – 11
254 "Hope" is the thing with feathers – 11
258 There's a certain Slant of light, 12
271 A solemn thing – it was – I said – 13
273 He put the Belt around my life – 13
274 The only Ghost I ever saw 14
280 I felt a Funeral, in my Brain, 15

285 The Robin's my Criterion for Tune –   15
288 I'm Nobody! Who are you?   16
291 How the old Mountains drip with Sunset   16
303 The Soul selects her own Society –   17
311 It sifts from Leaden Sieves –   18
312 Her – "last Poems" –   19
315 He fumbles at your Soul   19
320 We play at Paste –   20
322 There came a Day at Summer's full,   20
324 Some keep the Sabbath going to Church –   21
326 I cannot dance upon my Toes –   22
327 Before I got my eye put out   23
338 I know that He exists.   23
341 After great pain, a formal feeling comes –   24
365 Dare you see a Soul *at the White Heat?*   25
374 I went to Heaven –   25
378 I saw no Way – The Heavens were stitched –   26
389 There's been a Death, in the Opposite House,   26
391 A Visitor in Marl –   27
401 What Soft – Cherubic Creatures –   28
414 'Twas like a Maelstrom, with a notch,   28
425 Good Morning – Midnight –   29
435 Much Madness is divinest Sense –   30
441 This is my letter to the World   30
448 This was a Poet – It is That   30
449 I died for Beauty – but was scarce   31
451 The Outer – from the Inner   32
454 It was given to me by the Gods –   32
462 Why make it doubt – it hurts it so –   33
465 I heard a Fly buzz – when I died –   33
475 Doom is the House without the Door –   34
479 She dealt her pretty words like Blades –   34
486 I was the slightest in the House –   35
489 We pray – to Heaven –   36
492 Civilization – spurns – the Leopard!   36
501 This World is not Conclusion.   37

Fascicle 17

348 I dreaded that first Robin, so, 38
505 I would not paint – a picture – 39
506 He touched me, so I live to know 40
349 I had the Glory – that will do – 40
507 She sights a Bird – she chuckles – 41
350 They leave us with the Infinite. 41
508 I'm ceded – I've stopped being Theirs – 42
509 If anybody's friend be dead 42
510 It was not Death, for I stood up, 43
511 If you were coming in the Fall, 44
351 I felt my life with both my hands 45
352 Perhaps I asked too large – 46
328 A Bird, came down the Walk – 46
512 The Soul has Bandaged moments – 47
513 Like Flowers, that heard the news of Dews, 48
    [*End of Fascicle 17*]
518 Her sweet Weight on my Heart a Night 48
520 I started Early – Took my Dog – 49
528 Mine – by the Right of the White Election! 50
536 The Heart asks Pleasure – first – 50
544 The Martyr Poets – did not tell – 50
546 To fill a Gap 51
547 I've seen a Dying Eye 51
569 I reckon – when I count at all – 52
570 I could die – to know – 52
572 Delight – becomes pictorial – 53
575 "Heaven" has different Signs – to me – 53
581 I found the words to every thought 54
585 I like to see it lap the Miles – 54
587 Empty my Heart, of Thee – 55
593 I think I was enchanted 56
599 There is a pain – so utter – 57
601 A still – Volcano – Life – 57
606 The Trees like Tassels – hit – and swung – 58

607   Of nearness to her sundered Things   59
613   They shut me up in Prose –   60
617   Don't put up my Thread and Needle –   60
627   The Tint I cannot take – is best –   61
640   I cannot live with You –   62
642   Me from Myself – to banish –   64
646   I think to Live – may be a Bliss   64
650   Pain – has an Element of Blank –   65
657   I dwell in Possibility –   66
670   One need not be a Chamber – to be Haunted –   66
675   Essential Oils – are wrung –   67
690   Victory comes late –   67
709   Publication – is the Auction   68
711   Strong Draughts of Their Refreshing Minds   69
712   Because I could not stop for Death –   69
721   Behind Me – dips Eternity –   70
728   Let Us play Yesterday –   71
741   Drama's Vitallest Expression is the Common Day   72
754   My Life had stood – a Loaded Gun –   73
762   The Whole of it came not at once –   74
784   Bereaved of all, I went abroad –   74
797   By my Window have I for Scenery   75
824   The Wind begun to knead the Grass –
        The Wind begun to rock the Grass   76
861   Split the Lark – and you'll find the Music –   77
875   I stepped from Plank to Plank   78
889   Crisis is a Hair   78
909   I make His Crescent fill or lack –   79
985   The Missing All – prevented Me   79
986   A narrow Fellow in the Grass   80
1021   Far from Love the Heavenly Father   81
1071   Perception of an object costs   81
1072   Title divine – is mine!   81
1129   Tell all the Truth but tell it slant –   82
1263   There is no Frigate like a Book   82
1304   Not with a Club, the Heart is broken   83

1311 This dirty – little – Heart   83
1412 Shame is the shawl of Pink   84
1498 Glass was the street – in tinsel Peril   84
1515 The Things that never can come back, are several –   85
1545 The Bible is an antique Volume –   85
1551 Those – dying then,   86
1562 Her Losses make our Gains ashamed –   86
1593 There came a Wind like a Bugle –   86
1598 Who is it seeks my Pillow Nights –   87
1601 Of God we ask one favor,   87
1651 A Word made Flesh is seldom   88
1670 In Winter in my Room   88
1705 Volcanoes be in Sicily   90
1732 My life closed twice before its close –   90

Notes   91

Note on the Author and Editor

EMILY DICKINSON was born in the United States in 1830, the second child of Edward Dickinson, a lawyer and politician in the western Massachusetts town of Amherst. Unusually for a young woman of the period, she received a challenging education in the modern curriculum of co-educational Amherst Academy. She then went on to study at Mount Holyoke Female Seminary, one of the first degree-granting institutions for women, but she returned home after one year. Except for visits to Washington, Philadelphia, and Boston, Dickinson spent the rest of her life at home in Amherst. She enjoyed a passionate friendship with her sister-in-law Susan Gilbert Dickinson, who was the preferred first reader of her poetry, and in the early 1860s she suffered some emotional torment, possibly connected to a figure she called the 'Master'. But it is the story told by the poetry which is the story worth reading.

Dickinson began writing poetry seriously in the late 1850s, and during her flood period of 1862–3 (also a time of crisis for the nation, plunged into a bitter Civil War) she was writing more than a poem a day. Her refusal to compromise her highly condensed expression and idiosyncratic punctuation meant that her works were mangled by editors until she withdrew from the 'auction' of publication. At the time of her death in 1886 only about one per cent of her 1,775 known poems had been published. In 1955 an accurate edition finally appeared.

The strongest influences on Dickinson's poetry are the Bible and Shakespeare. As a religious sceptic since adolescence in a community whose social and spiritual life was based on churchgoing and revivalism, she wrote many poems about being shut out of a lost heaven. As an innovative woman poet in a male literary culture, she sought out literary 'sisters': Elizabeth Barrett Browning, the Brontës, George Eliot, George Sand. She herself has in turn become a guiding figure for recent women's writing. One of the two great nineteenth-century American poets (together with Walt Whitman), Dickinson looks startlingly modern today: her pure, fierce complexity seems the missing link between the metaphysical poetry of the seventeenth century and the fragmented demands of the modern.

HELEN McNEIL is the author of the critical and biographical study *Emily Dickinson* (Virago and Pantheon, 1986). Amongst other critical works and broadcasts, she has published on Elizabeth Bishop and Sylvia Plath (Plath explicitly acknowledged her debt to Dickinson). An American who has worked in Britain for some years, she is a lecturer in American Literature at the University of East Anglia. She edited Edith Wharton's short stories, *Souls Belated and Other Stories* for Everyman.

Chronology of Dickinson's Life

Year	Age	Life
1830		Emily Dickinson born 10 December in Amherst, Massachusetts, USA, the second child, after Austin (1829–95), of lawyer Edward Dickinson and Emily Norcross Dickinson
1833	3	Lavinia ('Vinnie') her sister born (d. 1899)
1840	10	Grandfather Dickinson moves to Ohio; Edward sells his half of the family home, The Homestead, and the family move to another house in Amherst. Emily and Lavinia enter Amherst Academy, where students are taught a 'modern' curriculum including astronomy and pre-Darwinian geology
1842	12	Her father elected State Senator; re-elected 1843

Chronology of her Times

Year	Literary Context	Historical Events
1830	Stendhal, *Le Rouge et le noir*	Revolutionary uprisings in central Europe
		William IV King of England
		Louis-Philippe crowned
1831	Whittier, *Legends of New England*	Nat Turner's rebellion in Virginia
		Revolutions suppressed by Austria
1832	Death of Scott	President Andrew Jackson re-elected
	Death of Goethe	
1833	Balzac, *Eugenie Grandet*	Telegraph invented
1835	de Tocqueville, *Democracy in America*	John Quincy Adams elected President
1836	Ralph Waldo Emerson, 'Nature'	Texas declares independence
		People's Charter in England
1837	Emerson, 'The American Scholar'	Queen Victoria crowned
		Morse's electric telegraph
		American business collapse
1838	Poe, *Narrative of Arthur Gordon Pym*	First Atlantic steamships
1840	Dana, *Two Years Before The Mast*	Opium War
	Cooper, *The Pathfinder*	US population reaches 17 million
1841	Emerson, *Essays, First Series*	John Tyler elected President
1842	Longfellow, *Ballads and Other Poems*	Chartists' second petition
1843		Texas annexed from Mexico

Year	Age	Life
1846	16	Religious revival in Amherst; Dickinson expresses doubts to her friend Abiah Root
1847	17	Enters Mount Holyoke Female Seminary
1848	18	Withdraws from Mount Holyoke
1850	20	Another religious revival in Amherst; her father and Lavinia and her friend, Susan Gilbert (1830–1913), join First Church of Christ
1851	21	Travels with her sister to Boston
1852	22	Her father, standing as a conservative Whig candidate, is elected to the US House of Representatives
1853	23	Amherst–Belchertown railway opens, promoted by her father
1854	24	Family visits Washington DC
1855	25	Visits Washington and Philadelphia with her sister Edward moves his family back into The Homestead; Dickinson will stay here for the rest of her life. Defeated in November's election, Edward sets up law partnership with Austin Health of mother declines; henceforth Dickinson and Lavinia run household

Year	Literary Context	Historical Events
1844	Dickens, *Martin Chuzzlewit*	Oregon boundary dispute between Britain and the US
	Emerson, *Essays, Second Series*	Telegraph line from Washington to Baltimore
1846	Melville, *Typee*	US-Mexico War
		Oregon settlement
1847	Thackeray, *Vanity Fair*	Mormons settle in Utah
	Emily Brontë, *Wuthering Heights*	Irish Potato Famine
	Longfellow, *Evangeline*	American troops occupy Mexico
	Charlotte Brontë, *Jane Eyre*	
1848	Death of Emily Brontë	Mexico cedes Texas and California to US
	Lowell, *Poems and Biglow Papers*	California Gold Rush
1849	Thoreau, 'Civil Disobedience'	Zachary Taylor elected President
	Parkman, *The Oregon Trail*	
	Death of Poe	
1850	Hawthorne, *The Scarlet Letter*	Death of President Taylor
	Tennyson, *In Memoriam*	US population reaches 23 million
		Fugitive Slave Law passed
1851	Melville, *Moby Dick*	*Coup d'état* in Paris
1852	Stowe, *Uncle Tom's Cabin*	
1853	Dickens, *Bleak House*	Franklin Pierce elected President
		Railway from New York to Chicago
1854	Thoreau, *Walden*	Kansas–Nebraska Act
	Dickens, *Hard Times*	Outbreak of the Crimean War
1855	Whitman, *Leaves of Grass*	
	Longfellow, *Song of Hiawatha*	
	Death of Charlotte Brontë	

Year	Age	Life
1856	26	Austin joins First Church and marries Susan Gilbert who becomes intimate friend of Dickinson's
1857	27	Emerson lectures in Amherst and stays with Austin and Susan; Dickinson does not attend and gradually begins to withdraw from society
1858	28	Writing poetry seriously
1859	29	Meets Catherine (Kate) Scott (later Anthon); they are close friends for six years
1860	30	Rev Charles Wadsworth visits her
1861	31	*Springfield Republican* prints poem 'I taste a liquor never brewed' altered and titled 'The May-Wine'
1862	32	In 1862–3 writes about 300 poems but undergoes a personal crisis. Shares Amherst's grief for loss of men killed in the Civil War Thomas Wentworth Higginson discourages her from publishing her poems
1864	34	In Boston for seven months for eye treatment. Two more poems printed
1865	35	About a thousand poems written by the end of this year
1866	36	*Springfield Republican* prints 'A narrow Fellow in the Grass' in a much-altered form
1867	37	Austin supervises building of new First Church opposite his house
1872	42	Edward Dickinson resigns as Treasurer of Amherst College and Austin succeeds him
1873	43	Edward elected to Massachusetts House of Representatives as independent candidate
1874	44	Edward dies suddenly in Boston. Austin and Susan's third child Gilbert, born

Year	Literary Context	Historical Events
1856	Turgenev, *Rudin* Elizabeth Barrett Browning, *Aurora Leigh*	End of Crimean War James Buchanan elected President
1857	Flaubert, *Madame Bovary* Lowell, Editor, *Atlantic Monthly*	Indian Mutiny
1858		*Great Eastern* launched First marine cable to Europe
1859	Darwin, *On the Origin of Species*	Burning of Summer Palace, Beijing
1860	Death of Schopenhauer Eliot, *Mill on the Floss*	Abraham Lincoln elected President
1861	Dostoevsky, *Notes from the House of the Dead* Death of Elizabeth Barret Browning	Outbreak of American Civil War
1862		Homestead Act
1863	Tolstoy, *The Cossacks*	Emancipation proclamation Battle of Gettysburg
1864	Death of Hawthorne	General Sherman captures Savannah
1865	Kipling and Yeats born	Civil War ends Lincoln assassinated
1866	Dostoevsky, *Crime and Punishment*	Fourteenth Amendment Transatlantic cable laid Ulysses S. Grant elected President
1872	Eliot, *Middlemarch*	
1874	Frost, Lowell and Stein born	

Year	Age	Life
1875	45	Mother Emily henceforth bedridden with paralysis
1876	46	Helen Hunt Jackson (1830–85), Amherst-born poet, becomes literary friend and begs her to publish
1878	48	'Success is counted sweetest' published anonymously at Jackson's urging
		Samuel Bowles, editor of *Springfield Republican*, dies
1880	50	Judge Otis Lord calls frequently at The Homestead and discusses marriage but is turned down
1882	52	Mother Emily dies
		Rev Charles Wadsworth dies
		Austin begins long affair with Mabel Loomis Todd
1883	53	Nephew Gilbert dies
1884	54	Judge Lord dies
		First attack of kidney disease
1885	55	Helen Hunt Jackson dies
1886	55	Dies of kidney disease
1890		First selection of poetry published

Year	Literary Context	Historical Events
1876	Tolstoy, *Anna Karenina* Twain, *Tom Sawyer* Death of George Sand	Bell's speaking telephone Battle of Little Big Horn
1879	Ibsen, *A Doll's House*	Einstein and Stalin born
1880	Wallace Stevens born Dostoevsky, *The Brothers Karamazov*	Boer uprising in Transvaal
1881	James, *Portrait of a Lady*	
1882	Death of Emerson	
1885	Twain, *Huckleberry Finn* Howells, *The Rise of Silas Lapham*	Grover Cleveland elected President Statue of Liberty
1886	Ezra Pound born James, *The Bostonians*	Completion of Canadian Pacific Railway

Introduction

The poetry of Emily Dickinson seems to write itself before our eyes as work of the present. Direct, passionate and highly condensed, it has the immediacy of the modern. Yet Dickinson wrote in the middle of the nineteenth century: born in 1830 and writing most actively in the 1860s, she died in 1886, almost twenty-five years before Virginia Woolf decided that human nature had changed, and slightly longer until the poetic revolution of Imagism, which her work often anticipates. Dickinson wrote about some of the great Romantic and Victorian topics: love, loss, death, Nature and God, and she lived out the restricted life expected of a woman of good family in a New England town. The vital difference is that Dickinson didn't write about her topics as fixed or known entities. Her poetry and her letters look at every experience, every object, every emotion as if it were wholly new. Every word, every punctuation mark, even every word left out counts for something in Dickinson.

Titles can replace the process of experiencing the poem: Dickinson doesn't use them, and her poems are now usually referred to by number or by their first line. Punctuation, capitalization, slant rhyme and irregular metre were part of her poetic tools. When editors insisted on conventionalizing her work, she felt her poems 'robbed' from her and withdrew from publishing: 'Publication – is the Auction/ Of the Mind' (709). Only about one per cent of her 1,775 known poems were published during her lifetime. Abstractions often replace the felt experience of the real, in life as well as in poetry; Dickinson does use them occasionally, but mainly to anatomize or critique: ' "Heaven" – is what I cannot reach!' (239); 'Civilization – spurns – the Leopard!' (492). Dickinson is more interested in her Leopard: 'Tawny – her Customs . . . Spotted – her Dun Gown'.

If the habit of Victorian poets such as Tennyson and Swinburne was to envelop the reader or listener in a comforting blanket of language, then Dickinson tears that blanket and exposes us to her stark, distinct, jewel-like world. 'Bright Flowers slit a Calyx/ And

soared upon a Stem/ Like Hindered Flags' (606) she writes, creating
the detailed movement of a flower's thrust upwards into blossom.
'Twas like a Maelstrom, with a notch,/That nearer, every Day,/
Kept narrowing its boiling wheel' (414), she writes, combining
imagery of a whirlpool, a wheel of torture, and a boiling pot to
concentrate a precise sensation of agony. In an age of oratory with
'Much Gesture, from the Pulpit –' (501), she chose the near-
silence of the terse poetic script. The poems are short: a number are
only eight lines long. But they are a slow read, and the after-shocks
last indefinitely.

When Emily Dickinson was growing up in New England, the
United States still laboured under a sense of cultural inferiority to
Britain, even while it revelled in the freedom of being the 'first new
nation', a democratic republic. English writers such as Wordsworth, Keats and Dickens, and the Scot Burns, were all read eagerly
by Dickinson (though she disliked Wordsworth). Boston, New
England's largest city, was the cultural capital of the United States,
and its intellectual ferment gave rise to Tanscendentalism, a
literary and social movement which mingled European Romanticism, philosophical idealism, and religious and social reform.
Essays such as 'Nature', 'The American Scholar' and 'The Poet'
made Ralph Waldo Emerson the foremost cultural figure of his age,
but an ambiguous model for Dickinson, who tried out Emerson's
Orphic generalizations in some poems and sharply rejected them in
others. Henry David Thoreau's meticulous observations in *Walden*
parallel Dickinson's; Margaret Fuller, co-editor with Emerson of the
transcendentalist magazine *The Dial*, wrote the dashing feminist
tract *Woman in the Nineteenth Century*, Nathaniel Hawthorne
satirized Fuller cruelly in *The Blithedale Romance* (a warning to the
female intellectual), but his 1850 'romance' *The Scarlet Letter*
castigated the New England Puritan past for its persecution of
extraordinary women and its hostility to the heart. Dickinson
became a poet at a place and time when romanticism, a weakened
but still powerful Puritanism, and the emergent power of women all
converged.

Educated in the rigorous modern curriculum of co-educational
Amherst Academy, where she studied sciences as well as arts, and
then attending for one year Mount Holyoke Female Seminary, one
of the first degree-granting colleges for women in the world,
Dickinson was unusually well-prepared to play a cultural role;

her classmates became wives of ministers or lawyers, and one, Helen Hunt Jackson, became a popular writer who championed Dickinson's work. Dickinson became invisible, and sent her poems to friends or self-published them in folded-over booklets or 'fascicles' (this edition contains the entire Fascicle 17). Throughout her work a kind of investigative confidence, a wide-ranging vocabulary, and a high productivity stand in apparent contradiction to an imagery of anguished withdrawl.

Dickinson was an omnivorous reader all her life, devouring magazines, popular writing and new writing as well as the accepted canon. For her books are food, or a frigate or a 'frugal' 'Chariot/ That bears the Human soul' (1263). In her poetry and letters the most visible influences are the Bible and Shakespeare: these two central texts of literary English centre her work in turn. Shakespeare is used allusively, as when 'Ceaseless Rosemary' carries the scent of Ophelia, death and memory (675). Dickinson's beloved sister-in-law Susan Gilbert Dickinson is told, 'Egypt, thou knew'st –' in a coded reference where Sue is Cleopatra and Emily Anthony. The allusive phrase packs into the poem or letter a characterization or an image-based insight that may range through an entire play in the original. Dickinson's use of the King James (Authorized) version of the Bible, tends more towards direct quotes, whose import is restricted or altered. The Gospels and the Revelation of St John of Patmos act as a shorthand for sacrifice, passion, revelation. Other phrases are ironized after being set apart by inverted commas. Yet Dickinson was not a bookish writer. She didn't go through a phrase of writing imitations, and her poetry is not dependent upon learned reference. Shakespeare was her model for linguistic richness and he is absorbed into her work (she once reportedly remarked that no other book was needed). The Bible was common cultural currency, to be valued, traded, or devalued.

When lines from George Herbert's 'Matins' were found in Dickinson's handwriting after her death, her first editors thought she had written them herself. The homely imagery of emblem books like Quarles's *Emblems*, the spiritual eloquence of Sir Thomas Browne's *Religio Medici* (both of which Dickinson read) and American Puritan poets like Anne Bradstreet and the baroque Edward Taylor (almost certainly also read) all derive from the same biblical sources. Arguably these seventeenth-century writers and translators gave Dickinson her metaphysical love of paradox, her willingness to push metaphor to its limits in metaphysical conceit, and her sense of the physical world as a book of revelation. The meditative quest for wisdom animates the Dickinson poem, but her poems usually end on a modern note of surmise or doubt, marked by conditional verbs and a concluding dash.

Dickinson's uncanny resemblance to William Blake (whose *Songs of Innocence and Experience* weren't available for her to read) arises from their shared inheritance of radical Protestantism. For Dickinson, doubt and suffering are what 'gave me that precarious Gait/ Some call Experience' (875). For both writers, what Blake called the 'minute particulars' of the perceived world are hugely important, though of the two Dickinson is more likely to stay with the luminous detail. Both Blake and Dickinson also wrote in the deliberately humble, even childlike tetrameter hymn quatrains of Isaac Watts, meanwhile adapting and playing upon his conventional piety. Dickinson's doubts about religion didn't lead her to construct an alternative mythology, as Blake did, or to turn to classical myth, as Shelley did, although she notes crisply that in contrast to the Bible, 'Orpheus' sermon captivated – /It did not condemn –' (1545). Her subjectivity stays with the process, trying to pin down how our experience creates 'internal difference/ Where the Meanings, are' (258). This 'difference' places Dickinson close to twentieth-century poets who also looked back to the seventeenth century, such as the otherwise very different T. S. Eliot and Elizabeth Bishop.

What Dickinson sees, she sees clearly. Like her older contemporary Walt Whitman, she often sets the distinctness of the real against the fuzziness or trickery of the transcendent. Although she uses metaphor, she often chooses to display the comparative process at work by using simile. 'I would not talk, like Cornets' (505). Her work is striking for its use of the tropes of metonym and synecdoche. In synecdoche the part represents the whole. In metonym a type or instance represents the entity of which it is an example; it isn't analogous to or 'like' it. Geographical images such as 'Himmaleh' (252) (the Himalayas) are used this way by Dickinson. There seems an effort in this figurative language to preserve the integrity of the signifier. The object which is in the poem must be respected as itself rather than simply as an element in a comparison. Dickinson sets apart important objects or concepts by dashes, enthroning them in the midst of the poetic line. In her honouring of the humble object, and in her sense of poetic duty and work (the poem enhancing and replacing the woman's 'work' of needlework), Dickinson seems to me to initiate a possible American poetic of pragmatism, of seeing the world as it is, heightened through provisional figurative structures. There is something of this in Emerson, in William James, and in the line of modernist realism marked by Robert Frost, Marianne Moore and (again) Elizabeth Bishop. These are also the markers of post-Puritan New England culture. Dickinson is acutely aware of spatial proportions, and of specificity of place. 'The Robin's my Criterion for Tune –' (285) Dickinson writes pragmatically, because she grew up around robins, not nightingales. Everyone, even the Queen of England, 'discerns provincially', because everyone comes from a specific cultural and physical topography. In her case, inevitably, 'I see – New Englandly'.

Yet although Dickinson arose from a Puritan culture, in certain essential ways her thought is not 'Puritan'. She never accepted the doctrine of Original Sin, according to which all children of Eve are born sinful. Nor did she embrace the Calvinist division of human-kind between the many Reprobate sinners and the few Elect or Redeemed. The 'visible Saints', always church members, usually a rich and powerful male elite, were for Dickinson the fraudulently 'meek members of the Resurrection –' (216), blind even to the collapse of the universe. In the majority of her poems she is deliberately reprobate, likely to be excluded for the slightest murmur: 'Why – do they shut Me out of Heaven? / Did I sing – too loud?' (248). Some of her most bitterly sardonic poems attack a cruel God who traps us in a 'magic prison' of the imaginary until we have been trained to 'reprimand the Happiness/ That too competes with Heaven' (1601). Nor does 'election' guarantee bliss: 'Far from Love the Heavenly Father/ Leads the Chosen Child' (1021). Sometimes the critique is gentle, couched in the apparent inno-cence of Dickinson's child persona: 'Some keep the Sabbath going to Church/ I keep it, staying at Home –' (324). But the tension remains between the drive for happiness and a religion based upon sin.

To most twentieth-century readers, Dickinson's rage against the Law of the Father feels familiar. But she was attracted also to the feminized Christ of her era, as in the passionate fragment 'Jesus! thy Crucifix' (225). In her most Emersonian poems, the Nature we see is a symbol for the presence beyond: 'Apprehensions – are God's introductions –' (797). For Dickinson, each must have his own different 'Opinion' of the meaning of the 'Sea – with a Stem' that Dickinson sees from her window. For Emerson, particulars must flow together into the single transcendent symbol of the Emersonian Oversoul. Death is the moment when immortality is tested. In her struggle to know, Dickinson places her speaker at or, eerily, *beyond* the moment of death: 'I heard a Fly buzz – when I died –' (465). While the others at the deathbed await 'that last Onset – when the King/ Be witnessed – in the Room –', Dickinson elides part of the verb: '*will* be witnessed'? '*may* be witnessed'? to make the case conditional. The drive to know death can arouse an almost sadistic curiosity: 'I like a look of Agony/ Because I know it's true –' (241). When Dickinson inverts the gendered Romantic theme of Death and the Maiden by giving the maiden a voice, the result is an uncanny convergence of wit and terror: 'Because I could not stop for Death – / He kindly stopped for me –' (712). The poem may also be a riposte to her contemporary Edgar Allan Poe, whose gothic tales she found excessive.

Women writers in the nineteenth century were expected to conform to appropriately feminine topics and to express genteel attitudes. The ones who broke out were heroines, 'sisters', 'queens', for Dickinson, who was almost as interested in their lives as their works. The third largest group of allusions in Dickinson is to the poetry of Elizabeth Barrett Browning, especially *Aurora Leigh*, her novel in verse about female creativity. When Barrett Browning died in 1861. Dickinson wrote three homages, 'Her – "last Poems" –' (312) and the famous 'I died for Beauty – but was scarce' (449) in which Barrett Browning is mingled with Keats references and with Dickinson herself as 'kinsmen' who have died for Truth and Beauty. 'I think I was enchanted' (593) is Dickinson's credo as a woman writer. Having read 'that Foreign Lady' 'When first a sombre Girl', Dickinson's speaker finds the world transformed 'For very Lunacy of Light'. Offered 'The Danger to be Sane', Dickinson turns instead 'To Tomes of solid Witchcraft', identifying herself with the witches persecuted by the New England Puritans, and with their work, the female poetic texts. Dickinson admired George Eliot: ('Her Losses make our Gains ashamed –' (1562) she wrote in 1882 after Eliot's death,) also George Sand, Harriet Beecher Stowe and the Brontë sisters. Probably the closest nineteenth-century parallel to Dickinson poems of anguish such as 'I felt a Funeral, in my Brain' (280) or

'Pain – has an Element of Blank –' (650) is the breakdown endured by Charlotte Brontë's heroine Lucy Snowe in *Villette*.

In an 1862 letter to her sometime literary 'preceptor' Thomas Wentworth Higginson, Dickinson warned against reading her poetry personally: 'When I state myself, as the Representative of the Verse – it does not mean – me – but a supposed person'. Dickinson seeks to avoid the author–reader intimacy of Romanticism, and asks for an almost modernist distancing of her speaker. In some poems the Dickinson 'I' (her most frequently used word after 'a' and 'the') is a mask or persona performing the act of the poem. 'I'm Nobody! Who are you?' In a number of poems Dickinson miniaturizes herself: 'I was the littlest in the house', or she wears the mask of the innocent or false-naive little girl: 'The little tippler/ Leaning against the – Sun –' (214). In the past, Higginson's anecdotes, the prevalence of the 'girl' poems in early anthologies, and the knowledge that Dickinson never married combined with the cultural assumption that women writers only write about themselves to create a false Dickinson of personal pleading, a shy little woman dressed in white. Only recently has this figure been dislodged, though the fruitless game of hunt-the-lover, in which I myself have taken part elsewhere, continues apace.

The beloved of the poems and of the abject letter-drafts known as the 'Master' letters may have been Samuel Bowles, editor of the *Springfield Republican*; it may have been the charismatic preacher Rev Charles Wadsworth, or it may have been 'sweet Sue', her sister-in-law and Dickinson's lifelong preferred first audience for her poems. There is certainly one poem expressing lesbian desire for a 'Bride': 'Her sweet Weight on my Heart a Night' (518). Or it may have been Kate Scott (Anthon). What must be remembered is while the beloved of the biographical Emily Dickinson may have been one or some or even all of these people, in the poem the love-object seen by the reader has been enlarged and set at an angle to whatever happened in life by the speculative strengthening of emotions that constitutes lyric poetry. Just as the novelist assembles character from mixtures of friends, people observed, and literary characters, amplifying, suppressing or inventing traits to make the picture sharper, so the lyric poet uses the raw material of biography as the starting point for greater or lesser transformations. Since no poem, no linguistic structure, can ever convey precisely an emotional state or 'be' an emotion that it is not, no speaker is ever precisely the author. Dickinson sent the same apparently intimate and personal poems to more than one recipient: some poems have versions for 'Him' and 'Her', and some poems have a male speaker. Even in the intensely personal poems of Sylvia Plath, who once wrote to her mother that any similarities between her poems and those of Dickinson were purely intentional, the stance of the speaker is worked up to fulfil the dramatic role assigned to it.

I have seen one of the notorious white dresses that Dickinson emblematically wore in her later years. It isn't a dress for a large woman, but it isn't small either. Size is something Dickinson the poet put on and took off, as in the astonishing shifts in proportions of so many poems. When we find ourselves attributing the feelings of the 'I' in a Dickinson poem to a real person, I suspect this is not so much Dickinson herself as ourselves, her readers, entering into the situation of the 'I' as we work through the poem's vividly imaged emotions. The 'I' of Dickinson's emotive poems is the agency not so much of a self as mere agency itself – the force driving the act of the poem, and then driven by the agency it has established. The tantalizing difficulty in establishing what many Dickinson poems are 'about' arises because the drive of the poem towards the process, rather than the goal. In poem 320, 'We play at Paste –', the lesson of learning value from the ordinary is clear; whether the 'Pearl' of the poem is love, heaven, poetic accomplishment or none of these, the process still applies equally. Dickinson knew, however, that in a patriarchal culture a poetics of pure agency had a price: agency for whom? In 'My life had stood – a Loaded Gun' (754) the speaker channels her explosively violent desire for expression into service for a Master: she is a gun, a volcano, a witch of 'Yellow Eye'. Yet when she has turned herself into her work she must recognize that 'I have but the power to kill,/ Without – the power to die –'

When Dickinson writes of joy, she uses active physical imagery. In the erotic 'luxury' of 'Wild Nights – Wild Nights!' (249), the speaker is the boat aiming for the port of the beloved. Once the port is known the journey itself is ecstatic; 'Rowing in Eden – / Ah, the Sea!' As in early mystical religions, she wants the ecstasy of revelation – particularly an erotic revelation – in this life, not the next: 'Dare you see a Soul *at the White Heat?*' (365). In 'Come slowly – Eden! (211) she is the 'fainting Bee' who in a Keatsian synaesthesia of the senses, sinks into the flower's nectar: 'Enters – and is lost in Balms'. One of Dickinson's most rewarding poems sets together the questing woman, the dissenter and the artist: 'I'm ceded – I've stopped being Theirs –' (508), she writes, adapting the language of secession of the Civil War raging in the American South. She discards the dolls, the sewing kit, and above all 'The name They dropped upon my face' when she lay 'Crowing – on my Father's breast –'. Instead, she embraces 'Existence's whole Arc, filled up'. Now, able to choose for herself, she chooses, with a lightly ironic arrogance, 'just' to be queen of herself and of her world: 'With Will to choose, or to reject,/ And I choose, just a Crown'.

HELEN McNEIL

A Note on This Text

Emily Dickinson published fewer than twenty poems during her lifetime (the number has risen gently as a result of recent intensive scholarship). Instead she sent her poems in letters and *as* letters, and she self-published by copying out her poems in eight-page booklets (called 'fascicles' by her editors), which she folded and bound herself. When she died her sister Lavinia discovered that hundreds of poems had been preserved in the fascicles and in manuscript; she took the poems to Susan Gilbert Dickinson, Dickinson's sister-in-law and preferred inner audience. After eighteen months of inaction, Lavinia retrieved the poems and offered them to Mabel Loomis Todd, who was the lover of Austin Dickinson, Emily and Lavinia's brother and Susan's husband. Mabel Loomis Todd brought in Dickinson's former literary mentor Thomas Wentworth Higginson, and they co-edited the 1890 *Selected Poems*. Higginson's comments established the public myth of Dickinson the eccentric recluse, and the edition altered words, added titles, regularized metre and 'corrected' punctuation, but it did bring Dickinson's work into view and it went through six editions. Other selections, some including Dickinson's sparkling letters, followed up until 1945.

Only in 1955, however, were Dickinson's poems finally published as she wrote them, without alterations to vocabulary, capitalization and punctuation. *The Complete Poems* edited by Thomas H. Johnson, has remained standard, and it is used for the text of almost all the poems in the present edition. Dickinson didn't, as a rule, title her poems, so Johnson numbered her poems in rough chronological order. This edition keeps Johnson's numbering for convenience, although it does *not* always print the poems in Johnson's sequence. To give a sense of how Dickinson organized and self-published her work in fascicles, this edition includes the complete Fascicle 17 (1862–3?) in Dickinson's original order as part of its selection. Dickinson continued to revise her poems after copying them into the fascicles or sending them to friends, and the revisions sometimes amount to substantial changes in meaning. Johnson's practice was to use the fascicle text without the revisions Dickinson added at the bottom of the page or on the line, but to prefer another text where that text was sent in a letter. When I have felt Dickinson's revisions amount to alternative readings, I have noted the revision, working from Carl Franklin's facsimiles in *The Manuscript Books of Emily Dickinson* (1981). To help the reader to follow Dickinson's creative process, I have also noted Dickinson's revisions to her poems in Fascicle 17.

Notes are to be found at the end of the collection, listed according to poem number.

Emily Dickinson

67

Success is counted sweetest
By those who ne'er succeed.
To comprehend a nectar
Requires sorest need.

Not one of all the purple Host   5
Who took the Flag today
Can tell the definition
So clear of Victory

As he defeated – dying –
On whose forbidden ear   10
The distant strains of triumph
Burst agonized and clear!

187

How many times these low feet staggered –
Only the soldered mouth can tell –
Try – can you stir the awful rivet –
Try – can you lift the hasps of steel!

Stroke the cool forehead – hot so often –   5
Lift – if you care – the listless hair –
Handle the adamantine fingers
Never a thimble – more – shall wear –

Buzz the dull flies – on the chamber window –
Brave – shines the sun through the freckled pane –   10
Fearless – the cobweb swings from the ceiling –
Indolent Housewife – in Daisies – lain!

193

I shall know why – when Time is over –
And I have ceased to wonder why –
Christ will explain each separate anguish
In the fair schoolroom of the sky –

He will tell me what "Peter" promised –
And I – for wonder at his woe –
I shall forget the drop of Anguish
That scalds me now – that scalds me now!

199

I'm "wife" – I've finished that –
That other state –
I'm Czar – I'm "Woman" now –
It's safer so –

How odd the Girl's life looks   5
Behind this soft Eclipse –
I think that Earth feels so
To folks in Heaven – now –

This being comfort – then
That other kind – was pain –   10
But why compare?
I'm "Wife"! Stop there!

211

Come slowly – Eden!
Lips unused to Thee –
Bashful – sip thy Jessamines –
As the fainting Bee –

Reaching late his flower,
Round her chamber hums –
Counts his nectars –
Enters – and is lost in Balms.

214

I taste a liquor never brewed –
From Tankards scooped in Pearl –
Not all the Vats upon the Rhine
Yield such an Alcohol!

Inebriate of Air – am I –   5
And Debauchee of Dew –
Reeling – thro endless summer days –
From inns of Molten Blue –

When 'Landlords' turn the drunken Bee
Out of the Foxglove's door –   10
When Butterflies – renounce their "drams" –
I shall but drink the more!

Till Seraphs swing their snowy Hats
And Saints – to windows run –
To see the little Tippler   15
Leaning against the – Sun –

216

Safe in their Alabaster Chambers –
Untouched by Morning
And untouched by Noon –
Sleep the meek members of the Resurrection –
Rafter of satin,   5
And Roof of stone.

Light laughs the breeze
In her Castle above them –
Babbles the Bee in a stolid Ear,
Pipe the Sweet Birds in ignorant cadence –   10
Ah, what sagacity perished here!

VERSION OF 1859

Safe in their Alabaster Chambers –
Untouched by Morning –
And untouched by Noon –
Lie the meek members of the Resurrection –   15
Rafter of Satin – and Roof of Stone!

Grand go the Years – in the Crescent – above them –
Worlds scoop their Arcs –
And Firmaments – row –
Diadems – drop – and Doges – surrender –   20
Soundless as dots – on a Disc of Snow –

VERSION OF 1861

225

Jesus! thy Crucifix
Enable thee to guess
The smaller size!

Jesus! thy second face
Mind thee in Paradise
Of ours!

228

Blazing in Gold and quenching in Purple
Leaping like Leopards to the Sky
Then at the feet of the old Horizon
Laying her spotted Face to die
Stooping as low as the Otter's Window
Touching the Roof and tinting the Barn
Kissing her Bonnet to the Meadow
And the Juggler of Day is gone

239

"Heaven" – is what I cannot reach!
The Apple on the Tree –
Provided it do hopeless – hang –
That – "Heaven" is – to Me!

The Color, on the Cruising Cloud –
The interdicted Land –

5

Behind the Hill – the House behind –
There – Paradise – is found!

Her teasing Purples – Afternoons –
The credulous – decoy –   10
Enamored – of the Conjuror –
That spurned us – Yesterday!

241

I like a look of Agony,
Because I know it's true –
Men do not sham Convulsion,
Nor simulate, a Throe –

The Eyes glaze once – and that is Death –
Impossible to feign
The Beads upon the Forehead
By homely Anguish strung.

243

I've known a Heaven, like a Tent –
To wrap its shining Yards –
Pluck up its stakes, and disappear –
Without the sound of Boards
Or Rip of Nail – Or Carpenter –   5
But just the miles of Stare –
That signalize a Show's Retreat –
In North America –

No Trace – no Figment of the Thing
That dazzled, Yesterday,   10

No Ring – no Marvel –
Men, and Feats –
Dissolved as utterly –
As Bird's far Navigation
Discloses just a Hue –   15
A plash of Oars, a Gaiety –
Then swallowed up, of View.

248

Why – do they shut Me out of Heaven?
Did I sing – too loud?
But – I can say a little "Minor"
Timid as a Bird!

Wouldn't the Angels try me –   5
Just – once – more –
Just – see – if I troubled them –
But don't – shut the door!

Oh, if I – were the Gentleman
In the "White Robe" –   10
And they – were the little Hand – that knocked –
Could – I – forbid?

249

Wild Nights – Wild Nights!
Were I with thee
Wild Nights should be
Our luxury!

Futile – the Winds –   5
To a Heart in port –
Done with the Compass –
Done with the Chart!

Rowing in Eden –
Ah, the Sea!   10
Might I but moor – Tonight –
In Thee!

250

I shall keep singing!
Birds will pass me
On their way to Yellower Climes –
Each – with a Robin's expectation –
I – with my Redbreast –   5
And my Rhymes –

Late – when I take my place in summer –
But – I shall bring a fuller tune –
Vespers – are sweeter than Matins – Signor –
Morning – only the seed of Noon –   10

251

Over the fence –
Strawberries – grow –
Over the fence –
I could climb – if I tried, I know –
Berries are nice!

But – if I stained my Apron –
God would certainly scold!
Oh, dear, – I guess if He were a Boy –
He'd – climb – if He could!

252

I can wade Grief –
Whole Pools of it –
I'm used to that –
But the least push of Joy
Breaks up my feet –   5
And I tip – drunken –
Let no Pebble – smile –
'Twas the New Liquor –
That was all!

Power is only Pain –   10
Stranded, thro' Discipline,
Till Weights – will hang –
Give Balm – to Giants –
And they'll wilt, like Men –
Give Himmaleh –   15
They'll Carry – Him!

254

"Hope" is the thing with feathers –
That perches in the soul –
And sings the tune without the words –
And never stops – at all –

And sweetest – in the Gale – is heard –   5
And sore must be the storm –
That could abash the little Bird
That kept so many warm –

I've heard it in the chillest land –
And on the strangest Sea –   10
Yet, never, in Extremity,
It asked a crumb – of Me.

258

There's a certain Slant of light,
Winter Afternoons –
That oppresses, like the Heft
Of Cathedral Tunes –

Heavenly Hurt, it gives us –   5
We can find no scar,
But internal difference,
Where the Meanings, are –

None may teach it – Any –
'Tis the Seal Despair –   10
An imperial affliction
Sent us of the Air –

When it comes, the Landscape listens –
Shadows – hold their breath –
When it goes, 'tis like the Distance   15
On the look of Death –

271

A solemn thing – it was – I said –
A woman – white – to be –
And wear – if God should count me fit –
Her blameless mystery –

A hallowed thing – to drop a life   5
Into the purple well –
Too plummetless – that it return –
Eternity – until –

I pondered how the bliss would look –
And would it feel as big –   10
When I could take it in my hand –
As hovering – seen – through fog –

And then – the size of this "small" life –
The Sages – call it small –
Swelled – like Horizons – in my vest –   15
And I sneered – softly – "small"!

273

He put the Belt around my life –
I heard the Buckle snap –
And turned away, imperial,
My Lifetime folding up –
Deliberate, as a Duke would do   5
A Kingdom's Title Deed –
Henceforth, a Dedicated sort –
A Member of the Cloud.

Yet not too far to come at call –
And do the little Toils   10

That make the Circuit of the Rest –
And deal occasional smiles
To lives that stoop to notice mine –
And kindly ask it in –
Whose invitation, know you not   15
For Whom I must decline?

274

The only Ghost I ever saw
Was dressed in Mechlin – so –
He wore no sandal on his foot –
And stepped like flakes of snow –

His Gait – was soundless, like the Bird –   5
But rapid – like the Roe –
His fashions, quaint, Mosaic –
Or haply, Mistletoe –

His conversation – seldom –
His laughter, like the Breeze –   10
That dies away in Dimples
Among the pensive Trees –

Our interview – was transient –
Of me, himself was shy –
And God forbid I look behind –   15
Since that appalling Day!

280

I felt a Funeral, in my Brain,
And Mourners to and fro
Kept treading – treading – till it seemed
That Sense was breaking through –

And when they all were seated,   5
A Service, like a Drum –
Kept beating – beating – till I thought
My Mind was going numb –

And then I heard them lift a Box
And creak across my Soul   10
With those same Boots of Lead, again,
Then Space – began to toll,

As all the Heavens were a Bell,
And Being, but an Ear,
And I, and Silence, some strange Race   15
Wrecked, solitary, here –

And then a Plank in Reason, broke,
And I dropped down, and down –
And hit a World, at every plunge,
And Finished knowing – then –   20

285

The Robin's my Criterion for Tune –
Because I grow – where Robins do –
But, were I Cuckoo born –
I'd swear by him –
The ode familiar – rules the Noon –   5
The Buttercup's, my Whim for Bloom –

Because, we're Orchard sprung –
But, were I Britain born,
I'd Daisies spurn –
None but the Nut – October fit –   10
Because, through dropping it,
The Seasons flit – I'm taught –
Without the Snow's Tableau
Winter, were lie – to me –
Because I see – New Englandly –   15
The Queen, discerns like me –
Provincially –

288

I'm Nobody! Who are you?
Are you – Nobody – Too?
Then there's a pair of us?
Don't tell! they'd advertise – you know!

How dreary – to be – Somebody!
How public – like a Frog –
To tell one's name – the livelong June –
To an admiring Bog!

291

How the old Mountains drip with Sunset
How the Hemlocks burn –
How the Dun Brake is draped in Cinder
By the Wizard Sun –

How the old Steeples hand the Scarlet   5
Till the Ball is full –

Have I the lip of the Flamingo
That I dare to tell?

Then, how the Fire ebbs like Billows –
Touching all the Grass   10
With a departing – Sapphire – feature –
As a Duchess passed –

How a small Dusk crawls on the Village
Till the Houses blot
And the odd Flambeau, no men carry   15
Glimmer on the Street –

How it is Night – in Nest and Kennel –
And where was the Wood –
Just a Dome of Abyss is Bowing
Into Solitude –   20

These are the Visions flitted Guido –
Titian – never told –
Domenichino dropped his pencil –
Paralyzed, with Gold –

303

The Soul selects her own Society –
Then – shuts the Door –
To her divine Majority –
Present no more –

Unmoved – she notes the Chariots – pausing –   5
At her low Gate –
Unmoved – an Emperor be kneeling
Upon her Mat –

I've known her – from an ample nation –
Choose One –   10
Then – close the Valves of her attention –
Like Stone –

311

It sifts from Leaden Sieves –
It powders all the Wood.
It fills with Alabaster Wool
The Wrinkles of the Road –

It makes an Even Face   5
Of Mountain, and of Plain –
Unbroken Forehead from the East
Unto the East again –

It reaches to the Fence –
It wraps it Rail by Rail   10
Till it is lost in Fleeces –
It flings a Crystal Vail

On Stump – and Stack – and Stem –
A Summer's empty Room –
Acres of Joints – where Harvests were,   15
Recordless but for them –

It Ruffles Wrists of Posts
As Ankles of a Queen –
Then stills its Artisans – like Ghosts –
Denying they have been –   20

312

Her – "last Poems" –
Poets – ended –
Silver – perished – with her Tongue –
Not on Record – bubbled other,
Flute – or Woman –   5
So divine –
Not unto its Summer – Morning
Robin – uttered Half the Tune –
Gushed too free for the Adoring –
From the Anglo-Florentine –   10
Late – the Praise –
'Tis dull – conferring
On the Head too High to Crown –
Diadem – or Ducal Showing –
Be its Grave – sufficient sign –   15
Nought – that We – No Poet's Kinsman –
Suffocate – with easy woe –
What, and if, Ourself a Bridegroom –
Put Her down – in Italy?

315

He fumbles at your Soul
As Players at the Keys
Before they drop full Music on –
He stuns you by degrees –
Prepares your brittle Nature   5
For the Ethereal Blow
By fainter Hammers – further heard –
Then nearer – Then so slow
Your Breath has time to straighten –
Your Brain -- to bubble Cool –   10

Deals – One – imperial – Thunderbolt –
That scalps your naked Soul –

When Winds take Forests in their Paws –
The Universe – is still –

320

We play at Paste –
Till qualified, for Pearl –
Then, drop the Paste –
And deem ourself a fool –

The Shapes – though – were similar –
And our new Hands
Learned *Gem*-Tactics –
Practicing *Sands* –

322

There came a Day at Summer's full,
Entirely for me –
I thought that such were for the Saints,
Where Resurrections – be –

The Sun, as common, went abroad,   5
The flowers, accustomed, blew,
As if no soul the solstice passed
That maketh all things new –

The time was scarce profaned, by speech –
The symbol of a word   10

Was needless, as at Sacrament,
The Wardrobe – of our Lord –

Each was to each The Sealed Church,
Permitted to commune this – time –
Lest we too awkward show   15
At Supper of the Lamb.

The Hours slid fast – as Hours will,
Clutched tight, by greedy hands –
So faces on two Decks, look back,
Bound to opposing lands –   20

And so when all the time had leaked,
Without external sound
Each bound the Other's Crucifix –
We gave no other Bond –

Sufficient troth, that we shall rise –   25
Deposed – at length, the Grave –
To that new Marriage,
Justified – through Calvaries of Love –

324

Some keep the Sabbath going to Church –
I keep it, staying at Home –
With a Bobolink for a Chorister –
And an Orchard, for a Dome –

Some keep the Sabbath in Surplice –   5
I just wear my Wings –
And instead of tolling the Bell, for Church,
Our little Sexton – sings.

God preaches, a noted Clergyman –
And the sermon is never long,   10

So instead of getting to Heaven, at last –
I'm going, all along.

326

I cannot dance upon my Toes –
No Man instructed me –
But oftentimes, among my mind,
A Glee possesseth me,

That had I Ballet knowledge –   5
Would put itself abroad
In Pirouette to blanch a Troupe –
Or lay a Prima, mad,

And though I had no Gown of Gauze –
No Ringlet, to my Hair,   10
Nor hopped to Audiences – like Birds,
One Claw upon the Air,

Nor tossed my shape in Eider Balls,
Nor rolled on wheels of snow
Till I was out of sight, in sound,   15
The House encore me so –

Nor any know I know the Art
I mention – easy – Here –
Nor any Placard boast me –
It's full as Opera –   20

327

Before I got my eye put out
I liked as well to see –
As other Creatures, that have Eyes
And know no other way –

But were it told to me – Today –   5
That I might have the sky
For mine – I tell you that my Heart
Would split, for size of me –

The Meadows – mine –
The Mountains – mine –   10
All Forests – Stintless Stars –
As much of Noon as I could take
Between my finite eyes –

The Motions of the Dipping Birds –
The Morning's Amber Road –   15
For mine – to look at when I liked –
The News would strike me dead –

So safer – guess – with just my soul
Upon the Window pane –
Where other Creatures put their eyes –   20
Incautious – of the Sun –

338

I know that He exists.
Somewhere – in Silence –
He has hid his rare life
From our gross eyes.

'Tis an instant's play.   5
'Tis a fond Ambush –
Just to make Bliss
Earn her own surprise!

But – should the play
Prove piercing earnest –   10
Should the glee – glaze –
In Death's – stiff – stare –

Would not the fun
Look too expensive!
Would not the jest –   15
Have crawled too far!

341

After great pain, a formal feeling comes –
The Nerves sit ceremonious, like Tombs –
The stiff Heart questions was it He, that bore,
And Yesterday, or Centuries before?

The Feet, mechanical, go round –   5
Of Ground, or Air, or Ought –
A Wooden way
Regardless grown,
A Quartz contentment, like a stone –

This is the Hour of Lead –   10
Remembered, if outlived,
As Freezing persons, recollect the Snow –
First – Chill – then Stupor – then the letting go –

365

Dare you see a Soul *at the White Heat?*
Then crouch within the door –
Red – is the Fire's common tint –
But when the vivid Ore
Has vanquished Flame's conditions,   5
It quivers from the Forge
Without a color, but the light
Of unanointed Blaze.
Least Village has its Blacksmith
Whose Anvil's even ring   10
Stands symbol for the finer Forge
That soundless tugs – within –
Refining these impatient Ores
With Hammer, and with Blaze
Until the Designated Light   15
Repudiate the Forge –

374

I went to Heaven –
'Twas a small Town –
Lit – with a Ruby –
Lathed – with Down –

Stiller – than the fields   5
At the full Dew –
Beautiful – as Pictures –
No Man drew.
People – like the Moth –
Of Mechlin – frames –   10
Duties – of Gossamer –
And Eider – names –
Almost – contented –

I – could be –
'Mong such unique   15
Society –

378

I saw no Way – The Heavens were stitched –
I felt the Columns close –
The Earth reversed her Hemispheres –
I touched the Universe –

And back it slid – and I alone –
A Speck upon a Ball –
Went out upon Circumference –
Beyond the Dip of Bell –

389

There's been a Death, in the Opposite House,
As lately as Today –
I know it, by the numb look
Such Houses have – alway –

The Neighbors rustle in and out –   5
The Doctor – drives away –
A Window opens like a Pod –
Abrupt – mechanically –

Somebody flings a Mattress out –
The Children hurry by –   10
They wonder if it died – on that –
I used to – when a Boy –

The Minister – goes stiffly in –
As if the House were His –
And He owned all the Mourners – now –   15
And little Boys – besides –

And then the Milliner – and the Man
Of the Appalling Trade –
To take the measure of the House –

There'll be that Dark Parade –   20

Of Tassels – and of Coaches – soon –
It's easy as a Sign –
The Intuition of the News –
In just a Country Town –

391

A Visitor in Marl –
Who influences Flowers –
Till they are orderly as Busts –
And Elegant – as Glass –

Who visits in the Night –   5
And just before the Sun –
Concludes his glistening interview –
Caresses – and is gone –

But whom his fingers touched –
And where his feet have run –   10
And whatsoever Mouth he kissed –
Is as it had not been –

401

What Soft – Cherubic Creatures –
These Gentlewomen are –
One would as soon assault a Plush –
Or violate a Star –

Such Dimity Convictions –   5
A Horror so refined
Of freckled Human Nature –
Of Deity – ashamed –

It's such a common – Glory –
A Fisherman's – Degree –   10
Redemption – Brittle Lady –
Be so – ashamed of Thee –

414

'Twas like a Maelstrom, with a notch,
That nearer, every Day,
Kept narrowing its boiling Wheel
Until the Agony

Toyed coolly with the final inch   5
Of your delirious Hem –
And you dropt, lost,
When something broke –
And let you from a Dream –

As if a Goblin with a Gauge –   10
Kept measuring the Hours –
Until you felt your Second
Weigh, helpless, in his Paws –

And not a Sinew – stirred – could help,
And sense was setting numb –   15
When God – remembered – and the Fiend
Let go, then, Overcome –

As if your Sentence stood – pronounced –
And you were frozen led
From Dungeon's luxury of Doubt   20
To Gibbets, and the Dead –

And when the Film had stitched your eyes
A Creature gasped "Reprieve"!
Which Anguish was the utterest – then –
To perish, or to live?   25

425

Good Morning – Midnight –
I'm coming Home –
Day – got tired of Me –
How could I – of Him?

Sunshine was a sweet place –   5
I liked to stay –
But Morn – didn't want me – now –
So – Goodnight – Day!

I can look – can't I –
When the East is Red?   10
The Hills – have a way – then –
That puts the Heart – abroad –

You – are not so fair – Midnight –
I chose – Day –
But – please take a little Girl –   15
He turned away!

435

Much Madness is divinest Sense –
To a discerning Eye –
Much Sense – the starkest Madness –
'Tis the Majority
In this, as All, prevail –
Assent – and you are sane –
Demur – you're straightway dangerous –
And handled with a Chain –

441

This is my letter to the World
That never wrote to Me –
The simple News that Nature told –
With tender Majesty

Her Message is committed
To Hands I cannot see –
For love of Her – Sweet – countrymen –
Judge tenderly – of Me

448

This was a Poet – It is That
Distills amazing sense
From ordinary Meanings –
And Attar so immense

From the familiar species

5

That perished by the Door –
We wonder it was not Ourselves
Arrested it – before –

Of Pictures, the Discloser –
The Poet – it is He –   10
Entitles Us – by Contrast –
To ceaseless Poverty –

Of Portion – so unconscious –
The Robbing – could not harm –
Himself – to Him – a Fortune –   15
Exterior – to Time –

449

I died for Beauty – but was scarce
Adjusted in the Tomb
When One who died for Truth, was lain
In an adjoining Room –

He questioned softly "Why I failed"?   5
"For Beauty", I replied –
"And I – for Truth – Themself are One –
We Brethren, are", He said –

And so, as Kinsmen, met a Night –
We talked between the Rooms –   10
Until the Moss had reached our lips –
And covered up – our names –

451

The Outer – from the Inner
Derives its Magnitude –
'Tis Duke, or Dwarf, according
As is the Central Mood –

The fine – unvarying Axis   5
That regulates the Wheel –
Though Spokes – spin – more conspicuous
And fling a dust – the while.

The Inner paints the Outer –
The Brush without the Hand –
Its Picture publishes – precise –
As is the inner Brand

On fine – Arterial Canvas –
A Cheek – perchance a Brow –
The Star's whole Secret – in the Lake –   15
Eyes were not meant to know.

454

It was given to me by the Gods –
When I was a little Girl –
They give us Presents most – you know –
When we are new – and small.
I kept it in my Hand –   5
I never put it down –
I did not care to eat – or sleep –
For fear it would be gone –
I heard such words as "Rich" –
When hurrying to school –   10
From lips at Corners of the Streets –

And wrestled with a smile.
Rich! 'Twas Myself – was rich –
To take the name of Gold –
And Gold to own – in solid Bars –   15
The Difference – made me bold –

462

Why make it doubt – it hurts it so –
So sick – to guess –
So strong – to know –
So brave – upon its little Bed
To tell the very last They said   5
Unto Itself – and smile – And shake –
For that dear – distant – dangerous – Sake –
But – the Instead – the Pinching fear
That Something – it did do – or dare –
Offend the Vision – and it flee –   10
And They no more remember me –
Nor ever turn to tell me why –
Oh, Master, This is Misery –

465

I heard a Fly buzz – when I died –
The Stillness in the Room
Was like the Stillness in the Air –
Between the Heaves of Storm –

The Eyes around – had wrung them dry –   5
And Breaths were gathering firm

For that last Onset – when the King
Be witnessed – in the Room –

I willed my Keepsakes – Signed away
What portion of me be   10
Assignable – and then it was
There interposed a Fly –

With Blue – uncertain stumbling Buzz –
Between the light – and me –
And then the Windows failed – and then   15
I could not see to see –

475

Doom is the House without the Door –
'Tis entered from the Sun –
And then the Ladder's thrown away,
Because Escape – is done –

'Tis varied by the Dream
Of what they do outside –
Where Squirrels play – and Berries die –
And Hemlocks – bow – to God –

479

She dealt her pretty words like Blades –
How glittering they shone –
And every One unbared a Nerve
Or wantoned with a Bone –

She never deemed – she hurt –   5
That – is not Steel's Affair –

A vulgar grimace in the Flesh –
How ill the Creatures bear –

To Ache is human – not polite –
The Film upon the eye   10
Mortality's old Custom –
Just locking up – to Die.

486

I was the slightest in the House –
I took the smallest Room –
At night, my little Lamp, and Book –
And one Geranium –

So stationed I could catch the Mint   5
That never ceased to fall –
And just my Basket –
Let me think – I'm sure
That this was all –

I never spoke – unless addressed –   10
And then, 'twas brief and low –
I could not bear to live – aloud –
The Racket shamed me so –

And if it had not been so far –
And any one I knew   15
Were going – I had often thought
How noteless – I could die –

489

We pray – to Heaven –
We prate – of Heaven –
Relate – when Neighbors die –
At what o'clock to Heaven – they fled –
Who saw them – Wherefore fly?   5

Is Heaven a Place – a Sky – a Tree?
Location's narrow way is for Ourselves –
Unto the Dead
There's no Geography –

But State – Endowal – Focus –   10
Where – Omnipresence – fly?

492

Civilization – spurns – the Leopard!
Was the Leopard – bold?
Deserts – never rebuked her Satin –
Ethiop – her Gold –
Tawny – her Customs –   5
She was Conscious –
Spotted – her Dun Gown –
This was the Leopard's nature – Signor –
Need – a keeper – frown?

Pity – the Pard – that left her Asia –   10
Memories – of Palm –
Cannot be stifled – with Narcotic –
Nor suppressed – with Balm –

501

This World is not Conclusion.
A Species stands beyond –
Invisible, as Music –
But positive, as Sound –
It beckons, and it baffles –   5
Philosophy – don't know –
And through a Riddle, at the last –
Sagacity, must go –
To guess it, puzzles scholars –
To gain it, Men have borne   10
Contempt of Generations
And Crucifixion, shown –
Faith slips – and laughs, and rallies –
Blushes, if any see –
Plucks at a twig of Evidence –   15
And asks a Vane, the way –
Much Gesture, from the Pulpit –
Strong Hallelujahs roll –
Narcotics cannot still the Tooth
That nibbles at the soul –   20

Fascicle 17

348

I dreaded that first Robin, so,
But He is mastered, now,
I'm some accustomed to Him grown,
He hurts a little, though –

I thought if I could only live   5
Till that first Shout got by –
Not all Pianos in the Woods
Had power to mangle me –

I dared not meet the Daffodils –
For fear their Yellow Gown   10
Would pierce me with a fashion
So foreign to my own –

I wished the Grass would hurry –
So – when 'twas time to see –
He'd be too tall, the tallest one   5
Could stretch – to look at me –

I could not bear the Bees should come,
I wished they'd stay away
In those dim countries where they go,
What word had they, for me?   20

They're here, though; not a creature failed –
No Blossom stayed away
In gentle deference to me –
The Queen of Calvary –

Each one salutes me, as he goes,   25
And I, my childish Plumes,

Lift, in bereaved acknowledgment
Of their unthinking Drums –

505

I would not paint – a picture –
I'd rather be the One
Its bright impossibility
To dwell – delicious – on –
And wonder how the fingers feel   5
Whose rare – celestial – stir –
Evokes so sweet a Torment –
Such sumptuous – Despair –

I would not talk, like Cornets –
I'd rather be the One   10
Raised softly to the Ceilings –
And out, and easy on –
Through Villages of Ether –
Myself endued Balloon
By but a lip of Metal –   15
The pier to my Pontoon –

Nor would I be a Poet –
It's finer – own the Ear –
Enamored – impotent – content –
The License to revere,   20
A privilege so awful
What would the Dower be,
Had I the Art to stun myself
With Bolts of Melody!

506

He touched me, so I live to know
That such a day, permitted so,
I groped upon his breast –
It was a boundless place to me
And silenced, as the awful sea　　　　　5
Puts minor streams to rest.

And now, I'm different from before,
As if I breathed superior air –
Or brushed a Royal Gown –
My feet, too, that had wandered so –　　　　10
My Gypsy face – transfigured now –
To tenderer Renown –

Into this Port, if I might come,
Rebecca, to Jerusalem,
Would not so ravished turn –　　　　15
Nor Persian, baffled at her shrine
Lift such a Crucifixal sign
To her imperial Sun.

349

I had the Glory – that will do –
An Honor, Thought can turn her to
When lesser Fames invite –
With one long "Nay" –
Bliss' early shape
Deforming – Dwindling – Gulfing up –
Time's possibility.

507

She sights a Bird – she chuckles –
She flattens – then she crawls –
She runs without the look of feet –
Her eyes increase to Balls –

Her Jaws stir – twitching – hungry –   5
Her Teeth can hardly stand –
She leaps, but Robin leaped the first –
Ah, Pussy, of the Sand,

The Hopes so juicy ripening –
You almost bathed your Tongue –   10
When Bliss disclosed a hundred Toes –
And fled with every one –

350

They leave us with the Infinite.
But He – is not a man –
His fingers are the size of fists –
His fists, the size of men –

And whom he foundeth, with his Arm   5
As Himmaleh, shall stand –
Gibraltar's Everlasting Shoe
Poised lightly on his Hand,

So trust him, Comrade –
You for you, and I, for you and me   10
Eternity is ample,
And quick enough, if true.

508

I'm ceded – I've stopped being Theirs –
The name They dropped upon my face
With water, in the country church
Is finished using, now,
And They can put it with my Dolls,   5
My childhood, and the string of spools,
I've finished threading – too –

Baptized, before, without the choice,
But this time, consciously, of Grace –
Unto supremest name –   10
Called to my Full – The Crescent dropped –
Existence's whole Arc, filled up,
With one small Diadem.

My second Rank – too small the first –
Crowned – Crowing – on my Father's breast –   15
A half unconscious Queen –
But this time – Adequate – Erect,
With Will to choose, or to reject,
And I choose, just a Crown –

509

If anybody's friend be dead
It's sharpest of the theme
The thinking how they walked alive –
At such and such a time –

Their costume, of a Sunday,   5
Some manner of the Hair –

A prank nobody knew but them
Lost, in the Sepulchre –

How warm, they were, on such a day,
You almost feel the date –   10
So short way off it seems –
And now – they're Centuries from that –

How pleased they were, at what you said –
You try to touch the smile
And dip your fingers in the frost –   15
When was it – Can you tell –

You asked the Company to tea –
Acquaintance – just a few –
And chatted close with this Grand Thing
That don't remember you –

Past Bows, and Invitations –
Past Interview, and Vow –
Past what Ourself can estimate –
That – makes the Quick of Woe!

510

It was not Death, for I stood up,
And all the Dead, lie down –
It was not Night, for all the Bells
Put out their Tongues, for Noon.

It was not Frost, for on my Flesh   5
I felt Siroccos – crawl –
Nor Fire – for just my Marble feet
Could keep a Chancel, cool –

And yet, it tasted, like them all,

The Figures I have seen   10
Set orderly, for Burial,
Reminded me, of mine –

As if my life were shaven,
And fitted to a frame,
And could not breathe without a key,   15
And 'twas like Midnight, some –

When everything that ticked – has stopped –
And Space stares all around –
Or Grisly frosts – first Autumn morns,
Repeal the Beating Ground –   20

But, most, like Chaos – Stopless – cool –
Without a Chance, or Spar –
Or even a Report of Land –
To justify – Despair.

511

If you were coming in the Fall,
I'd brush the Summer by
With half a smile, and half a spurn,
As Housewives do, a Fly.

If I could see you in a year,   5
I'd wind the months in balls –
And put them each in separate Drawers,
For fear the numbers fuse –

If only Centuries, delayed,
I'd count them on my Hand,   10
Subtracting, till my fingers dropped
Into Van Dieman's Land.

If certain, when this life was out –
That yours and mine, should be
I'd toss it yonder, like a Rind,   15
And take Eternity –

But, now, uncertain of the length
Of this, that is between,
It goads me, like the Goblin Bee –
That will not state – its sting.   20

351

I felt my life with both my hands
To see if it was there –
I held my spirit to the Glass,
To prove it possibler –

I turned my Being round and round   5
And paused at every pound
To ask the Owner's name –
For doubt, that I should know the Sound –

I judged my features – jarred my hair –
I pushed my dimples by, and waited –   10
If they – twinkled back –
Conviction might, of me –

I told myself, "Take Courage, Friend –
That – was a former time –
But we might learn to like the Heaven,   15
As well as our Old Home!"

352

Perhaps I asked too large –
I take – no less than skies –
For Earths, grow thick as
Berries, in my native town –

My Basket holds – just – Firmaments –
Those – dangle easy – on my arm,
But smaller bundles – Cram.

328

A Bird, came down the Walk –
He did not know I saw –
He bit an Angleworm in halves
And ate the fellow, raw,

And then, he drank a Dew   5
From a convenient Grass –
And then hopped sidewise to the Wall
To let a Beetle pass –

He glanced with rapid eyes
That hurried all around –   10
They looked like frightened Beads, I thought –
He stirred his Velvet Head

Like one in danger, Cautious,
I offered him a Crumb
And he unrolled his feathers   15
And rowed him softer home –

Than Oars divide the Ocean,
Too silver for a seam –

Or Butterflies, off Banks of Noon
Leap, plashless as they swim.   20

512

The Soul has Bandaged moments –
When too appalled to stir –
She feels some ghastly Fright come up
And stop to look at her –

Salute her – with long fingers –   5
Caress her freezing hair –
Sip, Goblin, from the very lips
The Lover – hovered – o'er –
Unworthy, that a thought so mean
Accost a Theme – so – fair –   10

The soul has moments of Escape –
When bursting all the doors –
She dances like a Bomb, abroad,
And swings upon the Hours,

As do the Bee – delirious borne –   15
Long Dungeoned from his Rose –
Touch liberty – then know no more,
But Noon, and Paradise –

The Soul's retaken moments –
When, Felon led along,   20
With shackles on the plumed feet,
And staples, in the Song,

The Horror welcomes her, again,
These, are not brayed of Tongue –

513

Like Flowers, that heard the news of Dews,
But never deemed the dripping prize
Awaited their – low Brows –

Or Bees – that thought the Summer's name
Some rumour of Delirium,   5
No Summer – could – for Them –

Or Arctic Creatures, dimly stirred –
By Tropic Hint – some Travelled Bird
Imported to the Word –

Or Wind's bright signal to the Ear –   10
Making that homely, and severe,
Contented, known, before –

The Heaven – unexpected come,
To Lives that thought the Worshipping
A too presumptuous Psalm –   15

                              END OF FASCICLE 17

518

Her sweet Weight on my Heart a Night
Had scarcely deigned to lie –
When, stirring, for Belief's delight,
My Bride had slipped away –

If 'twas a Dream – made solid – just   5
The Heaven to confirm –
Or if Myself were dreamed of Her –
The power to presume –

With Him remain – who unto Me –
Gave – even as to All –
A Fiction superseding Faith –
By so much – as 'twas real –

520

I started Early – Took my Dog –
And visited the Sea –
The Mermaids in the Basement
Came out to look at me –

And Frigates – in the Upper Floor   5
Extended Hempen Hands –
Presuming Me to be a Mouse –
Aground – upon the Sands –

But no Man moved Me – till the Tide
Went past my simple Shoe –   10
And past my Apron – and my Belt
And past my Bodice – too –

And made as He would eat me up –
As wholly as a Dew
Upon a Dandelion's Sleeve –   15
And then – I started – too –

And He – He followed – close behind –
I felt his Silver Heel
Upon my Ankle – Then my Shoes
Would overflow with Pearl –   20

Until We met the Solid Town –
No One He seemed to know –
And bowing – with a Mighty look –
At me – The Sea withdrew –

528

Mine – by the Right of the White Election!
Mine – by the Royal Seal!
Mine – by the Sign in the Scarlet prison –
Bars – cannot conceal!

Mine – here – in Vision – and in Veto!
Mine – by the Grave's Repeal –
Titled – Confirmed –
Delirious Charter!
Mine – long as Ages steal!

536

The Heart asks Pleasure – first –
And then – Excuse from Pain –
And then – those little Anodynes
That deaden suffering –

And then – to go to sleep –
And then – if it should be
The will of its Inquisitor
The privilege to die –

544

The Martyr Poets – did not tell –
But wrought their Pang in syllable –
That when their mortal name be numb –
Their mortal fate – encourage Some –

The Martyr Painters – never spoke –
Bequeathing – rather – to their Work –
That when their conscious fingers cease –
Some seek in Art – the Art of Peace –

546

To fill a Gap
Insert the Thing that caused it –
Block it up
With Other – and 'twill yawn the more –
You cannot solder an Abyss
With Air.

547

I've seen a Dying Eye
Run round and round a Room –
In search of Something – as it seemed –
Then Cloudier become –
And then – obscure with Fog –
And then – be soldered down
Without disclosing what it be
'Twere blessed to have seen –

569

I reckon – when I count at all –
First – Poets – Then the Sun –
Then Summer – Then the Heaven of God –
And then – the List is done –

But, looking back – the First so seems   5
To Comprehend the Whole –
The Others look a needless Show –
So I write – Poets – All –

Their Summer – lasts a Solid Year –
They can afford a Sun   10
The East – would deem extravagant –
And if the Further Heaven –

Be Beautiful as they prepare
For Those who worship Them –
It is too difficult a Grace –   15
To justify the Dream –

570

I could die – to know –
'Tis a trifling knowledge –
News-Boys salute the Door –
Carts – joggle by –
Morning's bold face – stares in the window –   5
Were but mine – the Charter of the least Fly –

Houses hunch the House
With their Brick Shoulders –
Coals – from a Rolling Load – rattle – how – near –
To the very Square – His foot is passing –   10

Possibly, this moment –
While I – dream – Here –

572

Delight – becomes pictorial –
When viewed through Pain –
More fair – because impossible
That any gain –

The Mountain – at a given distance –
In Amber – lies –
Approached – the Amber flits – a little –
And That's – the Skies –

575

"Heaven" has different Signs – to me –
Sometimes, I think that Noon
Is but a symbol of the Place –
And when again, at Dawn,

A mighty look runs round the World   5
And settles in the Hills –
An Awe if it should be like that
Upon the Ignorance steals –

The Orchard, when the Sun is on –
The Triumph of the Birds   10
When they together Victory make –
Some Carnivals of Clouds –

The Rapture of a finished Day –
Returning to the West –
All these – remind us of the place   15
That Men call "Paradise" –

Itself be fairer – we suppose –
But how Ourself, shall be
Adorned, for a Superior Grace –
Not yet, our eyes can see –   20

581

I found the words to every thought
I ever had – but One –
And that – defies me –
As a Hand did try to chalk the Sun

To Races – nurtured in the Dark –
How would your own – begin?
Can Blaze be shown in Cochineal –
Or Noon – in Mazarin?

585

I like to see it lap the Miles –
And lick the Valleys up –
And stop to feed itself at Tanks –
And then – prodigious step

Around a Pile of Mountains –   5
And supercilious peer

In Shanties – by the sides of Roads –
And then a Quarry pare

To fit its Ribs
And crawl between   10
Complaining all the while
In horrid – hooting stanza –
Then chase itself down Hill –

And neigh like Boanerges –
Then – punctual as a Star   15
Stop – docile and omnipotent
At its own stable door –

587

Empty my Heart, of Thee –
Its single Artery –
Begin, and leave Thee out –
Simply Extinction's Date –

Much Billow hath the Sea –   5
On Baltic – They –
Subtract Thyself, in play,
And not enough of me
Is left – to put away –
"Myself" meant Thee –   10

Erase the Root – no Tree –
Thee – then – no me –
The Heavens stripped –
Eternity's vast pocket, picked –

593

I think I was enchanted
When first a sombre Girl –
I read that Foreign Lady –
The Dark – felt beautiful –

And whether it was noon at night –   5
Or only Heaven – at Noon –
For very Lunacy of Light
I had not power to tell –

The Bees – became as Butterflies –
The Butterflies – as Swans   10
Approached – and spurned the narrow Grass –
And just the meanest Tunes

That Nature murmured to herself
To keep herself in Cheer –
I took for Giants – practising   15
Titanic Opera –

The Days – to Mighty Metres stept –
The Homeliest – adorned
As if unto a Jubilee
'Twere suddenly confirmed –   20

I could not have defined the change –
Conversion of the Mind
Like Sanctifying in the Soul –
Is witnessed – not explained –

'Twas a Divine Insanity   25
The Danger to be Sane
Should I again experience –
'Tis Antidote to turn –

To Tomes of solid Witchcraft –
Magicians be asleep –   30

But Magic – hath an Element
Like Deity – to keep –

599

There is a pain – so utter –
It swallows substance up –
Then covers the Abyss with Trance –
So Memory can step
Around – across – upon it –
As one within a Swoon –
Goes safely – where an open eye –
Would drop Him – Bone by Bone.

601

A still – Volcano – Life –
That flickered in the night –
When it was dark enough to do
Without erasing sight –

A quiet – Earthquake Style –   5
Too subtle to suspect
By natures this side Naples –
The North cannot detect

The Solemn – Torrid – Symbol –
The lips that never lie –   10
Whose hissing Corals part – and shut –
And Cities – ooze away –

606

The Trees like Tassels – hit – and swung –
There seemed to rise a Tune
From Miniature Creatures
Accompanying the Sun –

Far Psalteries of Summer –   5
Enamoring the Ear
They never yet did satisfy –
Remotest – when most fair

The Sun shone whole at intervals –
Then Half – then utter hid –   10
As if Himself were optional
And had Estates of Cloud

Sufficient to enfold Him
Eternally from view –
Except it were a whim of His   15
To let the Orchards grow –

A Bird sat careless on the fence –
One gossipped in the Lane
On silver matters charmed a Snake
Just winding round a Stone –   20

Bright Flowers slit a Calyx
And soared upon a Stem
Like Hindered Flags – Sweet hoisted –
With Spices – in the Hem –

'Twas more – I cannot mention –   25
How mean – to those that see –
Vandyke's Delineation
Of Nature's – Summer Day!

607

Of nearness to her sundered Things
The Soul has special times –
When Dimness – looks the Oddity –
Distinctness – easy – seems –

The Shapes we buried, dwell about,   5
Familiar, in the Rooms –
Untarnished by the Sepulchre,
The Mouldering Playmate comes –

In just the Jacket that he wore –
Long buttoned in the Mold   10
Since we – old mornings, Children – played –
Divided – by a world –

The Grave yields back her Robberies –
The Years, our pilfered Things –
Bright Knots of Apparitions   15
Salute us, with their wings –

As we – it were – that perished –
Themself – had just remained till we rejoin them –
And 'twas they, and not ourself
That mourned.   20

613

They shut me up in Prose –
As when a little Girl
They put me in the Closet –
Because they liked me "still" –

Still! Could themself have peeped –   5
And seen my Brain – go round –
They might as wise have lodged a Bird
For Treason – in the Pound –

Himself has but to will
And easy as a Star   10
Abolish his Captivity –
And laugh – No more have I –

617

Don't put up my Thread and Needle –
I'll begin to Sew
When the Birds begin to whistle –
Better Stitches – so –

These were bent – my sight got crooked –   5
When my mind – is plain
I'll do seams – a Queen's endeavor
Would not blush to own –

Hems – too fine for Lady's tracing
To the sightless Knot –   10
Tucks – of dainty interspersion –
Like a dotted Dot –

Leave my Needle in the furrow –
Where I put it down –

I can make the zigzag stitches   15
Straight – when I am strong –

Till then – dreaming I am sewing
Fetch the seam I missed –
Closer – so I – at my sleeping –
Still surmise I stitch –   20

627

The Tint I cannot take – is best –
The Color too remote
That I could show it in Bazaar –
A Guinea at a sight –

The fine – impalpable Array –   5
That swaggers on the eye
Like Cleopatra's Company –
Repeated – in the sky –

The Moments of Dominion
That happen on the Soul   10
And leave it with a Discontent
Too exquisite – to tell –

The eager look – on Landscapes –
As if they just repressed
Some Secret – that was pushing   15
Like Chariots – in the Vest –

The Pleading of the Summer –
That other Prank – of Snow –
That Cushions Mystery with Tulle,
For fear the Squirrels – know.   20

Their Graspless manners – mock us –
Until the Cheated Eye
Shuts arrogantly – in the Grave –
Another way – to see –

640

I cannot live with You –
It would be Life –
And Life is over there –
Behind the Shelf

The Sexton keeps the Key to –   5
Putting up
Our Life – His Porcelain –
Like a Cup –

Discarded of the Housewife –
Quaint – or Broke –   10
A newer Sevres pleases –
Old Ones crack –

I could not die – with You –
For One must wait
To shut the Other's Gaze down   15
You – could not –

And I – Could I stand by
And see You – freeze –
Without my Right of Frost –
Death's privilege?   20

Nor could I rise – with You –
Because Your Face
Would put out Jesus' –
That New Grace

Glow plain – and foreign   25
On my homesick Eye –
Except that You than He
Shone closer by –

They'd judge Us – How –
For You – served Heaven – You know,   30
Or sought to –
I could not –

Because You saturated Sight –
And I had no more Eyes,
For sordid excellence   35
As Paradise

And were You lost, I would be –
Though My Name
Rang loudest
On the Heavenly fame –   40

And were You – saved –
And I – condemned to be
Where You were not –
That self – were Hell to Me –

So We must meet apart –   45
You there – I – here –
With just the Door ajar
That Oceans are – and Prayer –
And that White Sustenance –
Despair –   50

642

Me from Myself – to banish –
Had I Art –
Impregnable my Fortress
Unto All Heart –

But since Myself – assault Me –   5
How have I peace
Except by subjugating
Consciousness?

And since We're mutual Monarch
How this be   10
Except by Abdication –
Me – of Me?

646

I think to Live – may be a Bliss
To those who dare to try –
Beyond my limit to conceive –
My lip – to testify –

I think the Heart I former wore   5
Could widen – till to me
The Other, like the little Bank
Appear – unto the Sea –

I think the Days – could every one
In Ordination stand –   10
And Majesty – be easier –
Than an inferior kind –

No numb alarm – lest Difference come –
No Goblin – on the Bloom –

No start in Apprehension's Ear,   15
No Bankruptcy – no Doom –

But Certainties of Sun –
Midsummer – in the Mind –
A steadfast South – upon the Soul –
Her Polar time – behind –   20

The Vision – pondered long –
So plausible becomes
That I esteem the fiction – real –
The Real – fictitious seems –

How bountiful the Dream –   25
What Plenty – it would be –
Had all my Life but been Mistake
Just rectified – in Thee

650

Pain – has an Element of Blank –
It cannot recollect
When it begun – or if there were
A time when it was not –

It has no Future – but itself –
Its Infinite contain
Its Past – enlightened to perceive
New Periods – of Pain.

657

I dwell in Possibility –
A fairer House than Prose –
More numerous of Windows –
Superior – for Doors –

Of Chambers as the Cedars –   5
Impregnable of Eye –
And for an Everlasting Roof
The Gambrels of the Sky –

Of Visitors – the fairest –
For Occupation – This –   10
The spreading wide my narrow Hands
To gather Paradise –

670

One need not be a Chamber – to be Haunted –
One need not be a House –
The Brain has Corridors – surpassing
Material Place –

Far safer, of a Midnight Meeting   5
External Ghost
Than its interior Confronting –
That Cooler Host.

Far safer, through an Abbey gallop,
The Stones a'chase –   10
Than Unarmed, one's a'self encounter –
In lonesome Place –

Ourself behind ourself, concealed –
Should startle most –

Assassin hid in our Apartment   15
Be Horror's least.

The Body – borrows a Revolver –
He bolts the Door –
O'erlooking a superior spectre –
Or More –   20

675

Essential Oils – are wrung –
The Attar from the Rose
Be not expressed by Suns – alone –
It is the gift of Screws –

The General Rose – decay –
But this – in Lady's Drawer
Make Summer – When the Lady lie
In Ceaseless Rosemary –

690

Victory comes late –
And is held low to freezing lips –
Too rapt with frost
To take it –
How sweet it would have tasted –   5
Just a Drop –
Was God so economical?
His Table's spread too high for Us –
Unless We dine on tiptoe –

Crumbs fit such little mouths –   10
Cherries – suit Robins –
The Eagle's Golden Breakfast strangles – Them –
God keep His Oath to Sparrows –
Who of little Love – know how to starve –

709

Publication – is the Auction
Of the Mind of Man –
Poverty – be justifying
For so foul a thing

Possibly – but We – would rather   5
From Our Garret go
White – Unto the White Creator –
Than invest – Our Snow –

Thought belong to Him who gave it –
Then – to Him Who bear   10
Its Corporeal illustration – Sell
The Royal Air –

In the Parcel – Be the Merchant
Of the Heavenly Grace –
But reduce no Human Spirit   15
To Disgrace of Price –

711

Strong Draughts of Their Refreshing Minds
To drink – enables Mine
Through Desert or the Wilderness
As bore it Sealed Wine –

To go elastic – Or as One
The Camel's trait – attained –
How powerful the Stimulus
Of an Hermetic Mind –

712

Because I could not stop for Death –
He kindly stopped for me –
The Carriage held but just Ourselves –
And Immortality.

We slowly drove – He knew no haste   5
And I had put away
My labor and my leisure too,
For His Civility –

We passed the School, where Children strove
At Recess – in the Ring –   10
We passed the Fields of Gazing Grain –
We passed the Setting Sun –

Or rather – He passed Us –
The Dews drew quivering and chill –
For only Gossamer, my Gown –   15
My Tippet – only Tulle –

We paused before a House that seemed
A Swelling of the Ground –

The Roof was scarcely visible –
The Cornice – in the Ground –   20

Since then – 'tis Centuries – and yet
Feels shorter than the Day
I first surmised the Horses' Heads
Were toward Eternity –

721

Behind Me – dips Eternity –
Before Me – Immortality –
Myself – the Term between –

Death but the Drift of Eastern Gray,
Dissolving into Dawn away,   5
Before the West begin –

'Tis Kingdoms – afterward – they say –
In perfect – pauseless Monarchy –
Whose Prince – is Son of None –
Himself – His Dateless Dynasty –   10
Himself – Himself diversify –
In Duplicate divine –

'Tis Miracle before Me – then –
'Tis Miracle behind – between –
A Crescent in the Sea –   15
With Midnight to the North of Her –
And Midnight to the South of Her –
And Maelstrom – in the Sky –

728

Let Us play Yesterday –
I – the Girl at school –
You – and Eternity – the
Untold Tale –

Easing my famine   5
At my Lexicon –
Logarithm – had I – for Drink –
'Twas a dry Wine –

Somewhat different – must be –
Dreams tint the Sleep –   10
Cunning Reds of Morning
Make the Blind – leap –

Still at the Egg-life –
Chafing the Shell –
When you troubled the Ellipse –   15
And the Bird fell –

Manacles be dim – they say –
To the new Free –
Liberty – Commoner –
Never could – to me –   20

'Twas my last gratitude
When I slept – at night –
'Twas the first Miracle
Let in – with Light –

Can the Lark resume the Shell –   25
Easier – for the Sky –
Wouldn't Bonds hurt more
Than Yesterday?

Wouldn't Dungeons sorer grate
On the Man – free –   30

Just long enough to taste –
Then – doomed new –

God of the Manacle
As of the Free –
Take not my Liberty   35
Away from Me –

741

Drama's Vitallest Expression is the Common Day
That arise and set about Us –
Other Tragedy

Perish in the Recitation –
This – the best enact   5
When the Audience is scattered
And the Boxes shut –

"Hamlet" to Himself were Hamlet –
Had not Shakespeare wrote –
Though the "Romeo" left no Record   10
Of his Juliet,

It were infinite enacted
In the Human Heart –
Only Theatre recorded
Owner cannot shut –   15

754

My Life had stood – a Loaded Gun –
In Corners – till a Day
The Owner passed – identified –
And carried Me away –

And now We roam in Sovereign Woods –   5
And now We hunt the Doe –
And every time I speak for Him –
The Mountains straight reply –

And do I smile, such cordial light
Upon the Valley glow –   10
It is as a Vesuvian face
Had let its pleasure through –

And when at Night – Our good Day done –
I guard My Master's Head –
'Tis better than the Eider-Duck's   15
Deep Pillow – to have shared –

To foe of His – I'm deadly foe –
None stir the second time –
On whom I lay a Yellow Eye –
Or an emphatic Thumb –   20

Though I than He – may longer live
He longer must – than I –
For I have but the power to kill,
Without – the power to die –

762

The Whole of it came not at once –
'Twas Murder by degrees –
A Thrust – and then for Life a chance –
The Bliss to cauterize –

The Cat reprieves the Mouse   5
She eases from her teeth
Just long enough for Hope to tease –
Then mashes it to death –

'Tis Life's award – to die –
Contenteder if once –   10
Than dying half – then rallying
For consciouser Eclipse –

784

Bereaved of all, I went abroad –
No less bereaved was I
Upon a New Peninsula –
The Grave preceded me –

Obtained my Lodgings, ere myself –   5
And when I sought my Bed –
The Grave it was reposed upon
The Pillow for my Head –

I waked to find it first awake –
I rose – It followed me –   10
I tried to drop it in the Crowd –
To lose it in the Sea –

In Cups of artificial Drowse
To steep its shape away –

The Grave – was finished – but the Spade   15
Remained in Memory –

797

By my Window have I for Scenery
Just a Sea – with a Stem –
If the Bird and the Farmer – deem it a "Pine" –
The Opinion will serve – for them –

It has no Port, nor a "Line" – but the Jays –   5
That split their route to the Sky –
Or a Squirrel, whose giddy Peninsula
May be easier reached – this way –

For Inlands – the Earth is the under side –
And the upper side – is the Sun –   10
And its Commerce – if Commerce it have –
Of Spice – I infer from the Odors borne –

Of its Voice – to affirm – when the Wind is within –
Can the Dumb – define the Divine?
The Definition of Melody – is –   15
That Definition is none –

It – suggests to our Faith –
They – suggest to our Sight –
When the latter – is put away
I shall meet with Conviction I somewhere met   20
That Immortality –

Was the Pine at my Window a "Fellow
Of the Royal" Infinity?
Apprehensions – are God's introductions –
To be hallowed – accordingly –   25

824

The Wind begun to knead the Grass –
As Women do a Dough –
He flung a Hand full at the Plain –
A Hand full at the Sky –
The Leaves unhooked themselves from Trees –   5
And started all abroad –
The Dust did scoop itself like Hands –
And throw away the Road –
The Wagons quickened on the Street –
The Thunders gossiped low –   10
The Lightning showed a Yellow Head –
And then a livid Toe –
The Birds put up the Bars to Nests –
The Cattle flung to Barns –
Then came one drop of Giant Rain –   15
And then, as if the Hands
That held the Dams – had parted hold –
The Waters Wrecked the Sky –
But overlooked my Father's House –
Just Quartering a Tree –   20

FIRST VERSION
c. 1864

The Wind begun to rock the Grass
With threatening Tunes and low –
He threw a Menace at the Earth –
A Menace at the Sky.

The Leaves unhooked themselves from Trees –   5
And started all abroad
The Dust did scoop itself like Hands
And threw away the Road.

The Wagons quickened on the Streets
The Thunder hurried slow –   10

The Lightning showed a Yellow Beak
And then a livid Claw.

The Birds put up the Bars to Nests –
The Cattle fled to Barns –
There came one drop of Giant Rain   15
And then as if the Hands

That held the Dams had parted hold
The Waters Wrecked the Sky,
But overlooked my Father's House –
Just quartering a Tree –   20

SECOND VERSION
c. 1864

861

Split the Lark – and you'll find the Music –
Bulb after Bulb, in Silver rolled –
Scantily dealt to the Summer Morning
Saved for your Ear when Lutes be old.

Loose the Flood – you shall find it patent –
Gush after Gush, reserved for you –
Scarlet Experiment! Sceptic Thomas!
Now, do you doubt that your Bird was true?

875

I stepped from Plank to Plank
A slow and cautious way
The Stars about my Head I felt
About my Feet the Sea.

I knew not but the next
Would be my final inch –
This gave me that precarious Gait
Some call Experience.

889

Crisis is a Hair
Toward which the forces creep
Past which forces retrograde
If it come in sleep

To suspend the Breath   5
Is the most we can
Ignorant is it Life or Death
Nicely balancing.

Let an instant push
Or an Atom press   10
Or a Circle hesitate
In Circumference

It – may jolt the Hand
That adjusts the Hair
That secures Eternity   15
From presenting – Here –

909

I make His Crescent fill or lack –
His Nature is at Full
Or Quarter – as I signify –
His Tides – do I control –

He holds superior in the Sky   5
Or gropes, at my Command
Behind inferior Clouds – or round
A Mist's slow Colonnade –

But since We hold a Mutual Disc –
And front a Mutual Day –   10
Which is the Despot, neither knows –
Nor Whose – the Tyranny –

985

The Missing All – prevented Me
From missing minor Things.
If nothing larger than a World's
Departure from a Hinge –
Or Sun's extinction, be observed –
'Twas not so large that I
Could lift my Forehead from my work
For Curiosity.

986

A narrow Fellow in the Grass
Occasionally rides –
You may have met Him – did you not
His notice sudden is –

The Grass divides as with a Comb –   5
A spotted shaft is seen –
And then it closes at your feet
And opens further on –

He likes a Boggy Acre
A Floor too cool for Corn –   10
Yet when a Boy, and Barefoot –
I more than once at Noon
Have passed, I thought, a Whip lash
Unbraiding in the Sun
When stooping to secure it   15
It wrinkled, and was gone –

Several of Nature's People
I know, and they know me –
I feel for them a transport
Of cordiality –   20

But never met this Fellow
Attended, or alone
Without a tighter breathing
And Zero at the Bone –

1021

Far from Love the Heavenly Father
Leads the Chosen Child,
Oftener through Realm of Briar
Than the Meadow mild.

Oftener by the Claw of Dragon
Than the Hand of Friend
Guides the Little One predestined
To the Native Land.

1071

Perception of an object costs
Precise the Object's loss –
Perception in itself a Gain
Replying to its Price –

The Object Absolute – is nought –
Perception sets it fair
And then upbraids a Perfectness
That situates so far –

1072

Title divine – is mine!
The Wife – without the Sign!
Acute Degree – conferred on me –
Empress of Calvary!
Royal – all but the Crown!

5

Betrothed – without the swoon
God sends us Women –
When you – hold – Garnet to Garnet –
Gold – to Gold –
Born – Bridalled – Shrouded –   10
In a Day –
Tri Victory
"My Husband" – women say –
Stroking the Melody –
Is *this* – the way?   15

1129

Tell all the Truth but tell it slant –
Success in Circuit lies
Too bright for our infirm Delight
The Truth's superb surprise

As Lightning to the Children eased
With explanation kind
The Truth must dazzle gradually
Or every man be blind –

1263

There is no Frigate like a Book
To take us Lands away
Nor any Coursers like a Page
Of prancing Poetry –
This Traverse may the poorest take
Without oppress of Toll –
How frugal is the Chariot
That bears the Human soul.

1304

Not with a Club, the Heart is broken
Nor with a Stone –
A Whip so small you could not see it
I've known

To lash the Magic Creature   5
Till it fell,
Yet that Whip's Name
Too noble then to tell.

Magnanimous as Bird
By Boy descried –   10
Singing unto the Stone
Of which it died –

Shame need not crouch
In such an Earth as Ours –
Shame – stand erect –   15
The Universe is yours.

1311

This dirty – little – Heart
Is freely mine.
I won it with a Bun –
A Freckled shrine –

But eligibly fair
To him who sees
The Visage of the Soul
And not the knees.

1412

Shame is the shawl of Pink
In which we wrap the Soul
To keep it from infesting Eyes –
The elemental Veil
Which helpless Nature drops
When pushed upon a scene
Repugnant to her probity –
Shame is the tint divine.

1498

Glass was the Street – in tinsel Peril
Tree and Traveller stood –
Filled was the Air with merry venture
Hearty with Boys the Road –

Shot the lithe Sleds like shod vibrations
Emphasized and gone
It is the Past's supreme italic
Makes this Present mean –

1515

The Things that never can come back, are several –
Childhood – some forms of Hope – the Dead –
Though Joys – like Men – may sometimes make a Journey –
And still abide –
We do not mourn for Traveler, or Sailor,   5
Their Routes are fair –
But think enlarged of all that they will tell us
Returning here –
"Here!" There are typic "Heres" –
Foretold Locations –   10
The Spirit does not stand –
Himself – at whatsoever Fathom
His Native Land –

1545

The Bible is an antique Volume –
Written by faded Men
At the suggestion of Holy Spectres –
Subjects – Bethlehem –
Eden – the ancient Homestead –   5
Satan – the Brigadier –
Judas – the Great Defaulter –
David – the Troubadour –
Sin – a distinguished Precipice
Others must resist –   10
Boys that "believe" are very lonesome –
Other Boys are "lost" –
Had but the Tale a warbling Teller –
All the Boys would come –
Orpheus' Sermon captivated –   15
It did not condemn –

1551

Those – dying then,
Knew where they went –
They went to God's Right Hand –
That Hand is amputated now
And God cannot be found –

The abdication of Belief
Makes the Behavior small –
Better an ignis fatuus
Than no illume at all –

1562

Her Losses make our Gains ashamed –
She bore Life's empty Pack
As gallantly as if the East
Were swinging at her Back.
Life's empty Pack is heaviest,
As every Porter knows –
In vain to punish Honey –
It only sweeter grows.

1593

There came a Wind like a Bugle –
It quivered through the Grass
And a Green Chill upon the Heat
So ominous did pass
We barred the Windows and the Doors   5

As from an Emerald Ghost –
The Doom's electric Moccasin
That very instant passed –
On a strange Mob of panting Trees
And Fences fled away   10
And Rivers where the Houses ran
Those looked that lived – that Day –
The Bell within the steeple wild
The flying tidings told –
How much can come   15
And much can go,
And yet abide the World!

1598

Who is it seeks my Pillow Nights –
With plain inspecting face –
"Did you" or "Did you not," to ask –
'Tis "Conscience" – Childhood's Nurse –

With Martial Hand she strokes the Hair
Upon my wincing Head –
"All" Rogues "shall have their part in" what –
The Phosphorus of God –

1601

Of God we ask one favor,
That we may be forgiven –
For what, he is presumed to know –
The Crime, from us, is hidden –
Immured the whole of Life

Within a magic Prison
We reprimand the Happiness
That too competes with Heaven.

1651

A Word made Flesh is seldom
And tremblingly partook
Nor then perhaps reported
But have I not mistook
Each one of us has tasted
With ecstasies of stealth
The very food debated
To our specific strength –

A Word that breathes distinctly
Has not the power to die
Cohesive as the Spirit
It may expire if He –
"Made Flesh and dwelt among us"
Could condescension be
Like this consent of Language
This loved Philology.

1670

In Winter in my Room
I came upon a Worm –
Pink, lank and warm –
But as he was a worm
And worms presume   5
Not quite with him at home –

Secured him by a string
To something neighboring
And went along.

A Trifle afterward   10
A thing occurred
I'd not believe it if I heard
But state with creeping blood –
A snake with mottles rare
Surveyed my chamber floor   15
In feature as the worm before
But ringed with power –

The very string with which
I tied him – too
When he was mean and new   20
That string was there –

I shrank – "How fair you are"!
Propitiation's claw –
"Afraid," he hissed
"Of me"?   25
"No cordiality" –
He fathomed me –
Then to a Rhythm *Slim*
Secreted in his Form
As Patterns swim   30
Projected him.

That time I flew
Both eyes his way
Lest he pursue
Nor ever ceased to run   35
Till in a distant Town
Towns on from mine
I set me down
This was a dream.

1705

Volcanoes be in Sicily
And South America
I judge from my Geography –
Volcanoes nearer here
A Lava step at any time
Am I inclined to climb –
A Crater I may contemplate
Vesuvius at Home.

1732

My life closed twice before its close –
It yet remains to see
If Immortality unveil
A third event to me

So huge, so hopeless to conceive
As these that twice befell.
Parting is all we know of heaven,
And all we need of hell.

Notes

Notes are listed according to the number of the poem. Proposed revisions by Dickinson are indicated by quotation marks.

187. **line 4** hasps: firm fastenings or latches. **line 7** adamantine: the hardest metal; diamonds; immovable or unbreakable

193. **line 5** In his First Epistle, the apostle Peter says: 'Ye are in heaviness through manifold temptations' but if you hope for grace and are faithful 'like obedient children' you will see Christ in Heaven (Peter1:6,1:14).

211. **line 3** Jessamines: jasmine, an intensely sweet-smelling flower. Dickinson often associates scent, honey and the more figurative 'balm', or soothing oil. See poems 252 and 492.

214. **line 3** 'Not all the Frankfort Berries'. **line 11** Drams, the Scots term for a measure of whisky, recalls Robert Burns, particularly 'Tam O'Shanter', in which Tam 'drinks divinely' with the landlady and landlord of an inn, but then must leave. **line 13** Seraphs, the six-winged angels who guard God's throne, strike fear into the prophet Isaiah (Isaiah 6:2-6). In her poetic drama 'The Seraphim' (1838), Elizabeth Barrett Browning has one seraph prefer the 'seraphic faces' of human inspiration to the glories of heaven. **line 16** 'From Manzanilla come'. Manzanilla is the centre of sherry production, just as the 'Franfort berries' locate a source for Rhine wine.

216. **line 4** A sardonic reference to the Calvinist (and thence Congregationalist) belief that only a few of the 'elect' will be saved by God's Covenant of Grace. The 'Alabaster Chambers' (**line 1**) of the members may also signal an attack on lawyers through the 'whited sepulchres' or hypocritical legal scribes denounced in Matthew 32:27. **line 20** The Doges were the elected rulers of the Republic of Venice for centuries until Napoleon abolished the Republic in 1797. **line 21**. Dickinson revised the poem to 'please you better – Sue'. When Sue still had doubts, she then offered a third version of the last stanza:

> Springs – shake the Sills –
> But – the Echoes – stiffen –
> Hoar – is the window –
> And numb – the door –
> Tribes of Eclipse – in Tents – of Marble –
> Staples – of Ages – have buckled – there –

241. line 7 To a nineteenth-century reader, the capitalized 'Agony' and the 'Beads upon the Forehead' would connect present psychological anguish and future death-pangs with the authenticity of Christ's 'agony' or struggle in the Garden of Gethsemane, when 'his sweat was as it were great drops of blood' (Luke 22:44–45).

248. line 10 St Peter is said to stand at the 'pearly gates' of Heaven. 'Knock, and it shall be opened to you,' says Luke 11:9, also Matthew 7:8.

250. line 9 Vespers are evening prayers, Matins are morning prayers. 'Signor' appears in several poems as a playful address to an apparently male authority or 'master'.

252. line 15 Himmaleh: the Himalaya mountains, here personifying massive power. See poem 350.

274. line 2 Mechlin: a type of raised lace embroidery traditionally made in Malines, France.

291. line 21 Guido: Guido Reni (1575–1642), Italian Baroque artist best known for his warm-toned pictures of saints and mythological scenes. **line 22** Titian: Tiziano Vecelli (1477–1576) Italian artist of the Venetian school, renowned for the grandeur of his work and for the tonal gradations of colour in his portraits and sacred and mythological scenes. **line 23** Domenichino: Domenico Veneziano (1400–1461) Italian artist known for his light, clear colour. None of these artists painted landscapes, except as background for figure compositions.

303. line 4 'Obtrude no more –'

311. line 12 'It deals Celestial Vail'. Johnson uses this alternative, found in a copy sent to Sue. **line 19** Booklet 29, where this poem appears, has 'Swans' with 'Ghosts' as an alternative. 'Ghosts' appears in the copy sent to Sue.

312. line 1 Reference to Elizabeth Barrett Browning (1806–61). After her death in June 1861 her husband, poet Robert Browning (1812–89), collected and published her *Last Poems* in February 1862. **Line 10** Anglo-Florentine: the Brownings were English, but lived in Florence after their elopement; Elizabeth Barrett Browning was actively involved in the cause of Italian liberty.

320. line 1 Paste: paste or imitation jewellery. **line 2** Pearl: the pearl, also, symbolically the 'pearl of great price' of Christ's transcendence and grace (Matthew 13:46). This image is used to express precious love in the fourteenth-century anonymous poem *Pearl*, and it is the name of Hester Prynne's daughter in Hawthrone's *The Scarlet Letter*.

322. line 4 The Visible Saints (or Elect) of Calvinism are those few who will be redeemed while others are damned. The many religious references in this poem have led to speculation that it is about, or for, Rev Charles Wadsworth, who became minister of Calvary Church, San Francisco, in April 1862. **line 13** The sealed Church: the chosen church, sealed or marked in Revelations 7:3–7, and unsealed by Christ 'the Lamb' on the Day of Judgement.

326. line 8 Prima: the prima donna or leading singer of grand opera.

341. line 6 Ought: aught, anything. **Lines 7 and 8** 'Regardless grown,/ A Wooden way'

391. line 1 Marl: heavy, clay-like earth, sometimes whitish; soft limestone.

401. line 5 Dimity: a puckered decorative cotton. **line 10** Reference to St Peter, who was a fisherman.

414. Dickinson builds on the imagery of Aurora's 'delirium' of grief: 'days, notched here and there with knives', in Elizabeth Barrett Brownings *Aurora Leigh* I, 215–22. The imagery also resembles Poe's 'Descent into the Maelstrom' and 'The Pit and the Pendulum'.

449. line 4 The poem expresses several homages. It is another tribute to the recently deceased Elizabeth Barrett Browning, who wrote in 'A Vision of Poets' (1838):

> These were poets true,
> Who died for Beauty, as martyrs do
> For Truth – the ends being scarcely two.

Both Dickinson and Browning refer to Keats's famous declaration in 'Ode on a Grecian Urn' (1818) that 'Beauty is truth, truth beauty.' The dialogic form of the poem resembles that of Robert Browning's *Men and Women* (1855).

492. line 4 Ethiop: Ethiopia, the African kingdom, where the Leopard is not 'rebuked' for her dark and golden beauty. **line 10** In fact the leopard (poetically 'pard') is native to Africa, not Asia.

348. This poem is the first of fifteen that Dickinson selected and bound together in this order in her seventeenth fascicle or booklet.

505. line 3 'Its fair impossibility' **line 7** 'Provokes so sweet a Torment –' **line 11** 'Raised softly to the Horizons' **line 12** 'And by, and easy on –' **line 14** Endued (endowed): several alternatives: upheld; upborne; sustained **line 21** 'A luxury so awful'

506. lines 2 and 3 'That such a day, persuaded so – I perished' and 'That such a day, accepted so – / dwell' **line 14** Rebecca, the wife of Isaac, died without arriving in Jerusalem. **line 16** Ancient Persians were Zoroastrians, worshipping the sun and its radiance.

507. line 5 'Her mouth stirs – longing – hungry –' **line 11**: 'When Bliss disclosed a hundred Wings –'

508. line 10 'Unto supremest term –' **line 12** 'Existence's whole Eye, filled up,' **line 13** 'With just one Diadem.' **line 15** 'Crowned – whimpering – on my Father's breast –', also 'Crowned – dangling – on my Father's breast –' **line 16** 'An insufficient Queen –' **line 18** 'With Power to choose, or to reject,' **line 19** 'And I choose, just a Throne –' The trope of self-crowning and self-naming may derive from Napoleon's crowning of himself as Emperor in 1803; Elizabeth Barrett Browning uses this image in her sonnet 'To George Sand: a Desire' when she praises the 'large brained woman and large-hearted man/ Self-called George Sand'. Sand was the pen name taken by Amandine-Aurore Lucille Dupin, influential French feminist romantic novelist (1804–76), and a heroine to both Dickinson and Browning. A self-crowning by a usurper takes place in Shakespeare's *Richard II*, when King Richard, in the opposite process, terrifyingly loses his identity when his 'name' and crown are taken away: 'No, not that name was given me at the font/But 'tis usurped.'

509. line 13 'How pleased they looked, at what you said – **line 14** 'You try to reach the smile' **line 15** 'And mix your fingers in the frost –' **line 23** 'Past what Oneself can understand'

510 Line 5 'It was not Frost, for on my Feet' **line 7** Nor Fire – for just two Marble feet –'

511. line 12 Van Dieman's Land: name of Tasmania until 1853. **line 16** 'And taste Eternity –'

328. line 3 'He bit an Angleworm in halves –

512. line 21 'With irons – on the plumed feet' **line 22** 'And rivets – in the Song'

520. line 12 'And past my Bosom – too –', also 'And past my Buckle – too –'

528. line 1 Again, the election of God's elect by the covenant of Grace. Possibly also the white smoke signalling the election of a new pope. Also references to the apocalypse and to legal contracts. **line 4** 'Bolts – cannot conceal!' **line 8** 'Good Affidavit!'

569. line 14 'For Those who Trust in Them –', also 'For those who Ask of Them –'

572. line 7 'Possessed – the Amber moves – a little –'

581. line 7 Cochineal: a scarlet red dye made from the cochineal insect. **line 8** Mazarin: a deep rich blue dye.

585. This riddle-poem has been variously connected with other contemporary reactions to the new technology of the railroad: Whitman's 'To a Locomotive in Winter', the 'Atropos' section of Henry David Thoreau's *Walden*, Charles Dickens's *The Uncommercial Traveller* and the train journey in Elizabeth Barrett Browning's *Aurora Leigh*, Book VII. Dickinson's father was one of the prime backers of the Amherst to Belchertown Railroad. **line 14** Boanerges: a fiery preacher especially one with a powerful voice; and a nickname applied by Jesus to James and John in Mark 3:17.

587. line 2 'Its Giant artery –' **line 6** Baltic: the sea separating Sweden from Germany and the Baltic states: a cold, northerly, enclosed sea.

593. line 3 Elizabeth Barrett Browning. The poem also alludes to the rather operatic *Aurora Leigh*. **line 29** Tomes: weighty volumes of magical female poetry. The persecution of women in the Puritan witch-hunts of late seventeenth-century Massachusetts left scars still felt in Dickinson's day. See Nathaniel Hawthorne, *The Scarlet Letter* (1850).

601. line 7 Inhabitants of Naples, who experience the smouldering volcano Vesuvius, may understand this 'Symbol', but colder, more northerly natures cannot. See poem 754.

606. line 5 Psalteries: psalters were books of psalms. **line 27** Vandyke: Sir Anthony Van Dyck (1599–1641), Flemish painter of dark-hued portraits, patronized by Charles I. As in poem 291, artistic representations, however famous, are 'mean' compared to Nature.

613. line 8 Pound: in the mid-nineteenth century, a roofless enclosure for stray animals: a place of containment and imprisonment.

627. line 7 Cleopatra: Queen of Egypt and lover of Mark Antony and Julius Caesar. The poem has the visual lushness of Shakespeare's *Antony and Cleopatra* without directly quoting it. On Cleopatra's barge:

> Ample the sails, and so perfumed that
> The winds were love-sick with them . . .
>   For her own person,
> It beggar'd all comparison (II, iii, 193–4, 197–8)

Later, when Antony has been defeated by Caesar after Cleopatra's navy (her 'company'?) has fled, he feels himself to have become illusory and shapeless, like a 'cloud that's dragonish/a vapour sometime, like a bear or lion' (IV, xiv, 3–4).

640. line 11 Sevres: French Sevres porcelain, highly regarded and of snob value.

642. This poem debating the sovereignty of consciousness uses the concept of the King's two bodies: inner or sanctified kingship (the divine right of kings) and the natural body of the King, explored by Shakespeare's *Richard II*. Rather than be usurped by Bolingbroke, Richard declares that 'I will undo myself' since only a king can undo kingship. But once he is no longer king: 'I have no name . . ./And know not now what to call myself' (IV, 1, 254ff). Shakespeare does not use the term 'abdication'. See also poems 508 and 528.

709. line 1 Publication: meaning here to voice abroad, to make public, as well as to print. 'Auction' may have echoes of the slave auction.

711. line 8 Hermetic: enclosed, complex, decipherable only by a few. Hermes Trismegistus (thrice great Hermes) was the Neoplatonist name for the Egyptian god Thoth, thought to be the same as the Greek god Hermes, presiding over mysticism, alchemy, and spiritual transformation. Dickinson is likely to have come across these ideas in the works of Sir Thomas Browne (1605–82); she had read his *Religio Medici*.

712. Dickinson reverses the point of view of the common Romantic theme of Death and the Maiden by giving voice to the woman. See Emily Brontë, 'No Coward Soul is Mine' and Robert Browning, 'The Last Ride Together'. **line 16** Tippet: a small wrap or stole made of wool. Tulle: a stiff netting, is a see-through material, as is gossamer, the stuff of cobwebs or, figuratively, the thinnest, most delicate fabric.

754. line 6 The masculine imagery of the heroic hunter was common in Dickinson's culture, as in James Fenimore Cooper's *The Deerslayer* (1841). The mountains' 'reply' to the retort of the gun brutally reworks the Romantic trope of nature corresponding to or echoing man's feelings. **line 18** 'None harm a second time' **line 19** Yellow Eye: the evil eye of a witch, also the flash of the gun firing. **line 23** 'For I have but the art to kill'

762. line 4 'The certain prey to tease –'

784. line 5 'Engrossed my Lodgings, ere myself –'

797. lines 22 and 23. Member of an elite group, such as a 'Fellow of the

Royal Society', formed to advance science in 1662. **line 25**. 'To be Extended inscrutably –'

861. line 7 'Sceptic Thomas' is the colloquial 'doubting Thomas' found in John 20: 25.

889. line 1 In the nineteenth century 'crisis' also meant the turning point of an illness.

1072. line 4 Calvary, the place of Christ's crucifixion, is seen by the speaker to be her empire. She is crowned, not with a diadem, but with (if anything) her personal Crown of Thorns. The poem was written about 1862 but not included in a booklet. See poems 322 and 348.

1545. line 7 Dickinson's satirical list reduces the Bible to a domestic melodrama, with Judas, the betrayer of Christ, merely a 'defaulter' on his debts. **line 8** David played the harp to comfort Saul (I Samuel 25); later he conquered Jerusalem. Here he is secularized into a troubadour, a medieval love poet. **line 15** Orpheus, son of the god Apollo in Greek myth, sang so beautifully that even trees and stones were moved.

1551. line 8 Ignis fatuus: delusive light, will o' the wisp, generated by gases in marshes and taken to be the lights of fires by unwary travellers.

1562. line 1 A homage to George Eliot (1819–80). Dickinson admired her poetry as well as her novels, and followed her life closely.

Everyman's Poetry

Titles available in this series

William Blake
ed. Peter Butter
0 460 87800 X

The Brontës
ed. Pamela Norris
0 460 87864 6

Rupert Brooke & Wilfred Owen
ed. George Walter
0 460 87801 8

Robert Browning
ed. Colin Graham
0 460 87893 X

Robert Burns
ed. Donald Low
0 460 87814 X

Lord Byron
ed. Jane Stabler
0 460 87810 7

Geoffrey Chaucer:
Comic and Bawdy Tales
ed. Malcolm Andrew
0 460 87869 7

John Clare
ed. R. K. R. Thornton
0 460 87823 9

Samuel Taylor Coleridge
ed. John Beer
0 460 87826 3

Emily Dickinson
ed. Helen McNeil
0 460 87895 6

John Donne
ed. D. J. Enright
0 460 87901 4

Four Metaphysical Poets
ed. Douglas Brooks-Davies
0 460 87857 3

Oliver Goldsmith
ed Robert L. Mack
0 460 87827 1

Thomas Gray
ed. Robert L. Mack
0 460 87805 0

Ivor Gurney
ed. George Walter
0 460 87797 6

Heinrich Heine
ed. T. J. Reed & David Cram
0 460 87865 4

George Herbert
ed. D. J. Enright
0 460 87795 X

Robert Herrick
ed. Douglas Brooks-Davies
0 460 87799 2

John Keats
ed. Nicholas Roe
0 460 87808 5

Henry Wadsworth Longfellow
ed. Anthony Thwaite
0 460 87821 2

Andrew Marvell
ed. Gordon Campbell
0 460 87812 3

John Milton
ed. Gordon Campbell
0 460 87813 1

More Poetry Please!
Foreword by P. J. Kavanagh
0 460 87899 9

Edgar Allan Poe
ed. Richard Gray
0 460 87804 2

Poetry Please!
Foreword by Charles Causley
0 460 87824 7

Alexander Pope
ed. Douglas Brooks-Davies
0 460 87798 4

Alexander Pushkin
ed. A. D. P. Briggs
0 460 87862 X

Lord Rochester
ed. Paddy Lyons
0 460 87819 0

Christina Rossetti
ed. Jan Marsh
0 460 87820 4

William Shakespeare
ed. Martin Dodsworth
0 460 87815 8

John Skelton
ed. Greg Walker
0 460 87796 8

R. L. Stevenson
ed. Jenni Calder
0 460 87809 3

Algernon Charles Swinburne
ed. Catherine Maxwell
0 460 87871 9

Alfred, Lord Tennyson
ed. Michael Baron
0 460 87802 6

Dylan Thomas
ed. Walford Davies
0 460 87831 X

Edward Thomas
ed. William Cooke
0 460 87877 8

R. S. Thomas
ed. Anthony Thwaite
0 460 87811 5

Walt Whitman
ed. Ellman Crasnow
0 460 87825 5

Oscar Wilde
ed. Robert Mighall
0 460 87803 4

W. B. Yeats
ed. John Kelly
0 460 87902 2